📞 01603 773114
email: tis@ccn.ac.uk 🐦 @CCN_Library Ⓦ ccnlibraryblog.wordpress.com
f /ccninformationstore

21 DAY LOAN ITEM

Please return <u>on or before</u> the last date stamped above

A fine will be charged for overdue items

CITY
COLLEGE
NORWICH

The Complete Guide to Teaching a Course
Ian Forsyth, Alan Jolliffe and David Stevens

Planning a Course
Preparing a Course
Delivering a Course
Evaluating a Course

The Complete Guide to **TEACHING a COURSE**

PREPARING
a course

2

Practical
Strategies
for
Teachers,
Lecturers
and Trainers

Ian Forsyth, Alan Jolliffe
and David Stevens

Second Edition

**KOGAN
PAGE**

First published in 1995
Second edition 1999

Kogan Page Limited
120 Pentonville Road
London N1 9JN
UK

Stylus Publishing Inc.
22883 Quicksilver Drive
Sterling, VA 20166
USA

© Ian Forsyth, Alan Jolliffe and David Stevens, 1995, 1999

British Library Cataloguing in Publication Data

A CIP record for this book is available from the British Library.

ISBN 0 7494 2808 2

Typeset by Jean Cussons Typesetting, Diss, Norfolk
Printed and bound in Great Britain by Biddles Ltd, Guildford and King's Lynn

Contents

Introduction   1

What each chapter covers   1
Who should read this book?   2

Chapter 1   Alternative Delivery Options   4
Summary   4
Introduction   4
How do you choose your delivery method?   4
Mass instruction   5
Group instruction   8
Individualized instruction 13
Teachers' roles   16
Conclusion   18

Chapter 2   Writing Distance Education Materials   19
Summary   19
Distance education   19
Course design   20
Planning to write the unit of work   25
Field trial   33
Conclusion   33

Chapter 3   Preparing Teaching Materials for Your Use   34
Summary   34
Introduction   34
Where do you start?   35
What is going to help you teach?   36
Some bottom line KIS (KISS)   39

Relating materials to the learners   44
Conclusion   44

**Chapter 4   Preparing Materials that
   Someone Else is Going to Teach   45**
Summary   45
Introduction   45
Types of teacher-independent materials: advantages
   and disadvantages   46
Items that make up teacher-independent materials   48
Preparing the learning event sheets   48
Conclusion   57

**Chapter 5   Criteria for Selecting
   Prepared Instructional Materials   59**
Summary   59
Introduction   59
The basic considerations   60
The steps in resource appraisal   61
Conclusion   68

**Chapter 6   Some Management Tips for a New Course
   or New Material   70**
Summary   70
Introduction   70
Two background organizational considerations   72
Some background on commercial production companies
   and in-house production units   73
Stages in developing your description of the materials you need   76
The pitfalls   78
Conclusion   80

Chapter 7   Innovation: Preparing the Materials   81
Summary   81
Introduction   81
Organizational culture   82
Cultural change   83
Overcoming the opposition   84
Changing attitudes   85
Case study   86
The learner   93
Conclusion   94

Chapter 8   Preparing On-line Learning Materials   95
Summary   95
Introduction   95
Developing learning materials   96
The on-line classroom   96
Client, server and support software   97
Connections   98
Design and development of an on-line learning system   100
Learning materials   100
Conclusion   104

Chapter 9   Issues of Access, Equity and Participation   105
Summary   105
Introduction   105
Access   106
Equity   106
Participation   107
Some initial or obvious problems   107
Problems in reality   108
Access, equity and participation: cultural issues   109
Access, equity and participation: technology   111
Where do I start?   112
Delivery options   114
Preparing learning materials   115
Conclusion   116

Chapter 10   The Independent Learner   117
Summary   117
Introduction   117
General uses of the term 'independent learner'   118
Promoting independence   119
Identification of needs   122
Enrolment and recognition of prior learning   122
Certification   122
Some words of warning   123
Conclusion   123

Chapter 11   Preparing to Deliver an Innovation   124
Summary   124
Introduction   124
Change   125
Time frames   125

Developing and maintaining support   126
The blocks   126
Induction   129
Conclusion   130

Further Reading   131

Index   133

Introduction

This book is the second in the series on planning, preparing, delivering and evaluating new courses and course material. In the planning book, the systematic collection of information about the course, the clients and the learners is considered: what the course is going to do, with whom, for what outcomes and with what resources.

In this book, the issues involved in preparing to deliver a course are addressed: 'generic' issues such as mode of delivery of a course, selecting pre-produced materials and dealing with the production of new course support materials, as well as issues of preparing both the learner and the community of the learner for the prospect of 'some other way of learning'. This book touches on issues of planning, delivery and evaluation, but its focus is on preparing for delivery in a variety of settings.

Additions to this book includes a chapter on the writing and developing of a distance learning course as well as an introduction to World Wide Web based learning. The Web is fast becoming all pervasive in the delivery of learning materials to the learner and it is important that you have at least a fundamental understanding of what the use of the Web means in the preparation of learning materials.

WHAT EACH CHAPTER COVERS

In Chapter 1 the various options of possible course delivery are discussed. In particular, the chapter looks at strategies such as open and flexible learning as alternate means for preparing the delivery of course material and opening up the learning process for the learner.

Chapter 2 provides you with a simple model to aid in the preparation of distance learning and self directed learning materials. The chapter also reviews the fundamentals of course design and describes the writing of a typical unit of work.

Chapter 3 discusses the preparation of teaching materials that you will use. The message here is very simple.

Chapter 4 discusses the preparation materials that others will use. The added complexity here is trying to maintain a 'uniformity' of presentation within a course taught by people with different teaching styles and amongst students with different learning styles.

In preparing to deliver a course, some material is already available as print, video, or computer-based information. In Chapter 5, there is a structured suggestion of how to evaluate this material to determine if it is suitable for your needs or the needs of the course.

Frequently the available material is out of date, or not suitable for the specific needs of the course. If you have gone through the processes outlined in Chapter 5, you will have at least some information to assist you in developing your own materials. This is outlined in Chapter 6.

Chapter 7 looks at some of the issues involved in change that you may have to address during the preparation stage.

Chapter 8 is a discussion surrounding the preparation of on-line and Web based learning materials. The chapter describes the typical on-line based classroom along with the various software and connections that need to be set up between client and the server. The chapter also covers learning requirements and materials production.

Chapter 9, on access, equity and participation, is no mere after-thought. The issues may have been addressed in the planning stage; the question now is how to address them in the preparation for delivery. It is not possible in a single chapter to detail all the options in planning, but it is possible to alert you to the possible need for options.

Chapter 10 follows on with a consideration of the need to encourage the activities of the independent learner. After all, the paradigm shift in education and training is from training for a job to lifelong learning.

The final chapter is about preparing to deliver: making sure that the planning and the preparation are 'deliverables'.

WHO SHOULD READ THIS BOOK?

The audience for this book is the classroom teacher, the trainer, the training unit manager, the learning materials developer and the project manager who has been asked to co-ordinate the development of learning materials.

There is also an assumption in this book that some planning has been undertaken to provide a viewpoint on the course or materials required.

There is also an assumption that the course and materials you want to develop reflect on the needs of the course, the learner, and/or provide a systematic and sanctioned means of delivery.

All the best for your preparation.

Ian Forsyth
Alan Jolliffe
David Stevens

Chapter 1
Alternative Delivery Options

SUMMARY

In this chapter the delivery methods available, using mass, group and individualized instruction, are discussed. The roles of both teachers and learners are described for each method of instruction.

INTRODUCTION

In a companion volume, *Planning a Course*, it was suggested that most teachers have a choice of three basic methods of instruction: mass, group and individualized. Within each category teachers have a wide choice of delivery methods. For example, the teacher may decide that the appropriate method of instruction for a particular 'set' of learning objectives is some form of individualized instruction. This instruction can be delivered in many ways, such as distance learning, flexible learning, resource-based learning, mastery learning, computer-based instruction or interactive video. All have the characteristics of individualized instruction and teachers must decide which is the most appropriate for their learners.

HOW DO YOU CHOOSE YOUR DELIVERY METHOD?

The choice is not simple and depends on a number of factors such as:

- the number of learners
- the type of learners – are they homogeneous?
- the type of content being taught
- how much time you have to develop the learning materials
- how often you teach the course
- the number of staff involved in teaching the course
- attitude of the staff
- the number and type of support staff you have available
- the type of educational environment you are working in
- the physical design of the learning environment
- the funds available to develop the course
- the administrative environment.

This chapter will assist you in deciding on the appropriate type of delivery method.

MASS INSTRUCTION

Mass instruction is a teacher-centred delivery method, where the teacher is the primary source of information. The lecture is a common mode of delivery and, although it may be delivered through broadcast television or video presentation, it is usually delivered live to large groups of learners. Large groups are defined as 30 or more learners, but there can be as many as 100 or even more. There is usually a one-way communication: the teacher talks.

Remember that mass instruction is teacher focused rather than learner focused, so use the strategy wisely.

The lecture is considered to be a traditional method of delivery, but it can be delivered in more interesting and interactive ways. Before we look at these, however, we should review the elements of an effective lecture.

Elements of an effective lecture

For a lecture to be effective it requires many elements and techniques to be incorporated into it. Some of these are:

- plan the lecture
- link the lecture to previous ones
- introduce the lecture
- state the aims and objectives clearly
- structure the content of the lecture
- present the content in a logical order

- emphasize the main points
- give the learners activities
- maintain the appropriate pace
- capture and maintain the learners' interest
- use questioning techniques
- maintain eye contact with the learners
- communicate clearly
- ensure the content is relevant and up-to-date
- be enthusiastic
- involve the learners in the lecture
- use repetition
- take into account a range of abilities
- monitor the learners' activities
- use teaching aids
- use examples and illustrations
- summarize the content
- evaluate the lecture
- evaluate the learners' learning
- use simple language
- gives notes and handouts.

There are many more factors to consider when giving a lecture, but this chapter is concerned with alternative delivery methods, so we will concentrate on ways of making your lecture more interactive by using different methods.

Interactive lectures

Make any lectures that you give as interactive as possible and put emphasis on the process of learning.

One of the many problems with lectures is that they tend to be content-based with too much emphasis on what is covered in the lecture rather than concentrating on how much the learners have actually learned. Making your lectures interactive is one method of making the learners become more involved and learn more effectively than just by listening, which is a passive form of learning. By making learners become more involved, the process of learning is given greater emphasis.

Many of the delivery methods described in group and individualized instruction can be applied to lectures to make them more interactive. The activities described in group instruction are particularly suitable for lectures, because lectures can be stopped and group activities can be applied.

Interactive lecture notes

Much of the learners' time during a lecture is spent taking notes; this is one method of getting and keeping them involved. Here learners must order the content, decide what is important and what should be included in the notes. However, there are a number of problems with learners taking notes, including:

Encourage learners to write all over the participant notes that you provide. One good way of doing this is to provide just a skeletal framework.

- the learners will spend most of their time in writing the notes and not thinking about what is being said in the lecture
- slow writers are disadvantaged
- learners with poor language skills are also disadvantaged
- each set of notes will be different; poor note-takers may fail to include important points
- complex diagrams and illustrations are difficult to copy correctly.

Because of these problems, many lecturers give lecture notes, but these, while solving some of the problems, create another set of problems. These include:

Don't fill participant notes up with too much detail. Try to leave lots for them to do as you are lecturing.

- learners will not make any notes, confident that everything is covered in the lecture notes
- in some cases it is important for learners to do the actual drawing, sketching, calculating and problem solving
- too much detail may be covered in the notes and obscure the important content
- if the learners know they will receive detailed notes they may not attend the lecture at all
- the learners may not pay attention, if they have detailed notes, making them more passive
- lecturers themselves may not be able to prepare effective notes.

Interactive lecture notes overcome many of the problems of having too-detailed notes by giving summary-type notes and activities which involve the learners. Below are some of the features of interactive notes:

Always try to include as many access devices as possible in your participant notes.

- state the objectives of the lecture; the learners then know the aims
- provide summary-type notes, in point form; the learners are then expected to add any details they think are important
- include revision activities which help the learners recall previous material covered

- leave blanks in the notes which the learners know they have to complete
- leave wide margins for students to make their own notes
- use partially completed diagrams and illustrations, which the learners are expected to complete or label
- include various types of questions. They can focus on the main ideas of the lecture, calculations, graphs, anything that involves the learners. The lectures should be stopped while the learners complete these questions
- provide access devices and advanced organizers, so the learners can find the relevant material and know what is coming up in the lecture. These include:
  - a sub heading structure
  - marginal notes
  - contents page
  - an index if a series of lectures are to be included in one book
- summaries can also be provided so that the learners have an overview of the material. Another useful activity is to leave the summary blank or partially completed so the learners can complete them
- include a reading list for the learners so that they can find additional information on the material covered in the lecture
- include a glossary of new words where the learners are expected to complete the meanings
- include revision questions at the end of the lecture.

Only lecture for 15 to 30 minutes at a time before having some form of activity.

Lectures have been used for a long time in education and will continue to be used in the future, even though there are many disadvantages. Using an effective lecturing technique, interactive notes and some of the activities explained in the sections on group and individualized instruction will make your lectures more effective.

GROUP INSTRUCTION

In the chapter on delivery options in a companion volume, *Planning a Course*, alternative delivery methods are discussed. The advantages of working in groups are also outlined. Group activities can be thought of as an alternative delivery method to those used in mass instruction.

Objectives of group work

The objectives of group work include:

- promoting discussion between the learners, with the teacher the discussion leader
- actively involving learners in the learning process
- assisting in the development of critical thinking, decision-making and problem-solving skills
- improving the oral communication of the learners
- increasing the motivation of the learners
- using the entire range of skills, knowledge, abilities and experience of the group
- allowing learners to learn from each other
- giving the learners experience in group dynamics
- allowing the learners to work independently of the larger group
- giving the learners opportunities to express their opinions and ideas
- encouraging the learners to take responsibility for their own learning
- allowing the learners to apply new skills.

How big is a group? Groups can be large or small and although the division is somewhat arbitrary, they are useful as guides.

Large groups include up to 30 learners, while smaller groups include a minimum of two and a maximum of six. Many of the delivery methods described are applicable to either large or small groups. When dealing with large groups, small group activities can be used, by simply breaking your large group into smaller groups. This does have

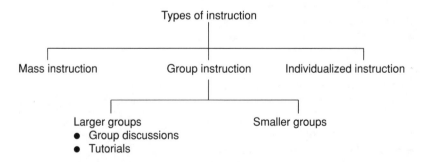

Figure 1.1 *Major types of group work*

the disadvantage of not having a teacher with every group and requires some independence on behalf of the learners.

In group work there is active participation by the learners and an attempt to cater for individual differences. The learners can work at the pace of the group rather than that of the larger numbers involved in mass instruction.

Group work is active learning. The more the learners are active, the more they will learn, so include active learning in your materials.

Large group work

There are two types of activities that fall into this class: classroom discussions and tutorials. Classroom discussion consists of the teacher lecturing for short periods of time, frequently questioning the learners for understanding and correcting any misunderstanding. The learners have the opportunity to ask questions at any stage and usually have frequent individual or group activities related to the topic under discussion. This method is commonly used in primary and secondary education.

Tutorials are used in conjunction with the lecture, where group size is usually less than the lectures. Tutorials focus on the information given in the lecture to explore problems, review cases, apply principles, undertake practice exercises, perform calculations and engage in discussions. The tutor is available to assist the learners and the learners can ask questions about the lectures which the lecturer did not have time to answer in the lecture.

Elements of an effective tutorial

There are many elements which make up an effective tutorial. An effective tutorial:

- should have objectives
- should not allow the tutor to talk too much
- should encourage the learners to ask questions and discuss problems
- is one where the learners should be made to feel comfortable in a physical sense. The environment may need to be changed to facilitate a discussion. The learners should feel relaxed about asking questions
- is where the course is taught in line with the objectives
- should assist the learners to learn
- should establish a rapport between the teachers and learners
- should involve the learners

- should allow for more personal attention to the learners than in lectures
- should allow the learners to work at their own pace.

Small group work

There are many different types of activities under the heading of small group work; some are shown in Figure 1.2. In most cases the teacher will have to coordinate a number of different groups during the class; their role changes to that of a group leader and coordinator of activities. The teacher must leave the learning process to the individual members of the group. Following is a discussion on some of the types of small group activities available.

Remember that in group work you become a guide and co-ordinator of learning rather than a 'teacher' who has all the right answers.

Seminars

Seminars are where small groups of learners prepare a paper or presentation on a topic selected by the teacher or themselves. The presentation is made to the larger group for discussion and analysis. Teachers play a less dominant role than in group discussions and coordinate, facilitate and make comments on the presentations.

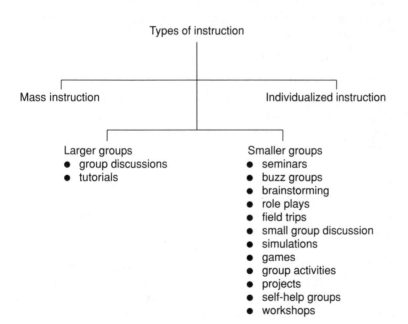

Types of instruction

Mass instruction

Individualized instruction

Larger groups
- group discussions
- tutorials

Smaller groups
- seminars
- buzz groups
- brainstorming
- role plays
- field trips
- small group discussion
- simulations
- games
- group activities
- projects
- self-help groups
- workshops

When using small group activities make sure the physical environment is flexible enough to support them.

Figure 1.2 *Types of small group work*

Buzz groups

The buzz group is given a problem or issue to discuss without the assistance of the teacher and asked to report back to the larger group.

Brainstorming

In brainstorming the teacher poses a problem and the learners suggest solutions. The other members of the group are not expected to comment on the solution. One member of the group records the solutions.

Role plays

Role plays are designed partially to replicate the real world. The larger group will have a discussion and from that a series of problems may be suggested. The smaller groups are asked to prepare a role play on one of the problems to demonstrate the problem. After the role play, the group analyses what has happened.

Field trips

The group or the teacher proposes the aim of the field trip and discusses how information will be collected and recorded, what format the report could take and how the project is to be evaluated. The learners then work in small groups to discuss the details of the trip to which the teachers must agree.

Small group discussion

Small group discussions allow the teacher to introduce ideas, issues, tasks and problems which small groups are formed to discuss. The teacher can guide the discussion through a series of questions to reach a conclusion.

Simulations

Simulations are an attempt to create the illusion of reality, where time, cost, danger, complexity or location preclude using the 'real' situation. They are often used in conjunction with games.

Games

Games are a type of competition played the learners with the object of winning within the rules of the games. Commercial games are widely used, but teachers can develop their own. Games enable the learners to make decisions in a risk-free environment. Games can involve role plays, simulations and case studies.

INDIVIDUALIZED INSTRUCTION

Individualized instruction is becoming increasingly important because of its many advantages, outlined in Chapter 6 of a companion volume, *Planning a Course*. Today's learners need and request a more flexible type of learning in a rapidly changing society. This type of learning can be delivered by individualized instruction.

There are a vast number of names given to different types of individualized learning, but most educators agree that they are all a type of open learning.

What is open learning?

Open learning is a method of delivering learning where learners use people, materials, equipment as their resources. In some cases, regular class attendance may not always be necessary. Any form of delivering learning that meets the above definition is said to be open.

The 'open' is open learning refers to learner-centred instruction where the needs of the learners are considered paramount. The learners have more control over their learning. Since instruction can be offered in a flexible manner it is often used to remove the barriers, such as course prerequisites, that prevent attendance on more traditional courses.

The characteristics of open learning courses include the following:

- the needs of the learners are paramount
- the learners may negotiate their own course pattern
- the learners have control over their learning
- it allows for self-pacing
- a variety of learning materials are used
- highly flexible modular courses; various forms of learning and styles of learning are catered for
- the teachers become facilitators
- there is some form of two-way communication between the learners and the teachers
- there is recognition of prior learning
- the enrolment procedure is more relaxed.

Not all open learning courses will have all of the above characteristics, but they should have a majority. In reality, you can never obtain a true open learning course, where learners can learn about any topic at any time. There will always be some type of restrictions, but in open learning they are kept to a minimum.

Today's learners need and often request a more flexible approach to the delivery of learning. In view of this you may want to consider converting your materials into a World Wide Web environment.

If you need a more flexible, learner centred way to deliver your learning materials, consider moving to an open learning environment.

When inplementing open learning, conduct your field trials on individual modules before implementing the entire course.

Distance education

Some teachers assume that the terms 'distance education' and 'open learning' can be used interchangeably, but this is not so.

Distance learning is a type of open learning, a method of delivering the learning where the student is geographically distant from the teacher and has to work independently within a structure.

Distance education depends heavily on print-based learning materials, while open learning materials may use different media, but it is the emphasis on learner-centred that distinguishes open from distance education, which can be closed and formal education.

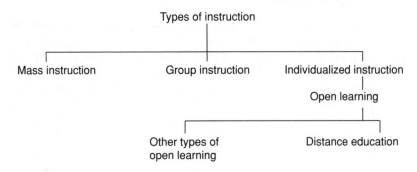

Figure 1.3   *Open learning and distance education*

When to use open learning

In a companion volume, *Planning a Course*, in the chapter on delivery options, we discussed the advantages and disadvantages of individualized instruction and how you would select the appropriate type of instruction. The following list outlines situations where open learning is suitable and situations where it is not.

You would use open learning where:
- there are a large number of learners to be trained
- the learners are geographically widespread
- new work or business methods are introduced and there is a shortage of specialists to train them
- remedial training is required
- training institutions are inaccessible
- consistent training is required, especially about processes
- waiting lists for face-to-face courses have developed

- flexibility in offering options is needed to make the training relevant to the learners
- continuity in training is required, especially when trainers change jobs and location
- learners do not want to attend courses
- self-pacing is important because of the heterogeneity of the learners
- training should be started immediately, rather than waiting for numbers to justify an attendance course to begin
- small numbers of learners become available for training over different periods of time.

You would not use open learning where:

- the learners' motivation is low, because open learning materials require considerable motivation and application
- motor skills training is the main part of the training (unless supportive attendance sessions can be added)
- the number of future learners is small
- socialization, change of attitude, meeting learners and interacting with other learners is important, eg, in some aspects of social work, health work, sales techniques and counselling
- the comparatively long time to develop the learning materials is not available
- there are not enough staff skilled in producing open learning materials
- there isn't enough cash to start and maintain the development and production of learning material
- management is not supportive of an open learning initiative
- the subject matter of the open learning course changes quickly.

So we can see that there are situations where open learning is applicable and some cases where it is not and other forms of instruction would be more suitable. The different types of open learning are shown in Figure 1.4.

If possible use an existing open learning package as a model or template and adapt it as necessary. You will save a lot of time doing it this way.

Open learning packages

Open learning packages are designed to assist the learners to learn without much assistance from the teacher. Packages are often print-based, but they can also use other media. The package is designed with a specific purpose in mind, it is aimed at specific learners and has specific objectives. Packages vary greatly; they could be made up of a

Figure 1.4　*Types of open learning*

textbook, learner's workbook and some other types of media such as audio or video cassettes. Teachers have the choice of developing their own packages, buying commercial ones or adapting existing ones. The development of learning materials will be discussed in more detail in the remaining chapters of this book.

TEACHERS' ROLES

In each of the types of instruction, the role of the teacher is different. In the lecture, teachers are the givers of information; in group instruction they are the facilitators; in open learning they are the tutors.

The role of teachers in mass instruction

Mass instruction is teacher-centred; teachers make most of the decisions about the instruction. Teachers usually decide on:

If you are going to 'teach' a course you should ensure that you are well prepared and the learning materials well planned.

- the contents of the course or session within the course
- the pace
- the teaching resources and
- the time and place of learning
- the role of the learner
- the ways the learners are instructed.

Learners have very little choice of how they will be taught in the teacher-centred method of instruction. The role of the teachers is as the controllers of knowledge and the givers of information.

The role of teachers in group instruction

The role of the teachers in group instruction is that of facilitator. They guide discussions and facilitate group learning activities.

    The role of the teacher can be divided into five classes:

Make sure that you are well prepared to work in a facilitative role and able to put 'being a teacher' to one side.

- leaders – where they lead the group
- consultants – where they are a resource to the learners
- facilitators – where they use the information or the comments of the learners
- participants – where they act as group members
- observers – where they act as an observer to the problems the groups tackle.

The role of teachers in individualized instruction

Individualized learning is a learner-centred method of instruction where the needs of the learners are paramount. The learners may not have complete control over all of the facets of instruction, depending on the type of delivery, but in a typical individualized instruction/learning situation the learners may have control of:

If you are considering moving to a learner-centred environment make sure that you are well prepared from a knowledge perspective and make sure you are ready to 'let go' and give control to others.

- the content of the course
- the pace of learning
- choice of learning resources used
- the time and place of learning.

The role of teachers in a learner-centred method of instruction is that of managers of the learning resources and facilitators of learning where they are available to assist the learners in their learning difficulties. They are supportive of the learners, as in a tutorial role. Teachers can be used as resources themselves.

Some teachers feel uncomfortable in anything other than a teacher-centred role; this is quite natural as they lose some control of the learners. However, experience will make teachers more comfortable in learner-centred instruction when they see that the learners can be given responsibility for their own learning.

CONCLUSION

Mass instruction delivery methods like the lecture can be made more effective by borrowing some of the techniques used in group and individual instruction. With the addition of 'good' lecturing techniques and interactive lecture notes the lecture can be made more effective. There are a large number of group instruction delivery methods the teacher can use to promote more learner-centred learning. Individualized instruction, which consists of open learning, has many techniques available and is becoming increasingly popular as a delivery method because it can deliver learning in a flexible manner which caters for the individual differences of the learners.

Chapter 2
Writing Distance Education Materials

SUMMARY

This chapter looks at the development of distance learning materials. Before you develop the learning materials you will need to decide on a course design and develop a learner profile. Once this is completed you should develop a model to assist you design the course. The individual components of the learning materials can then be designed to allow interaction as the materials are the major way the learners learn.

DISTANCE EDUCATION

Developing materials for distance learning is different from the development of other learning materials. Here the learners learn directly from the materials as there is no teacher to guide them. The learning materials replace the teacher as the deliverer of information, and the teacher has a new role, that of tutor. When developing distance education learning materials much more thought and work needs to be put into the design and preparation. This chapter explains in simple terms how to write distance education materials that are educationally sound in design. The principles are the same as those followed for the design of any self directed learning materials.

   Distance education is defined as a method of delivering the learning where the learners are geographically distant from the teacher and they have to work independently within a structure. This means the

Distance learning is a delivery method where the learners are geographically distant from you, so make sure that you design your materials with that in mind.

learning materials need to be well organized and developed in a systematic manner using the principles described in other chapters in this book series.

COURSE DESIGN

Your distance learning materials should be developed by a design team.

Usually, a distance education course is designed by a development team who work from a curriculum document that provides the broad outlines of the course. However, for small projects you may have to complete all the required tasks yourself.

A typical design development team is made up of instructional designer, subject matter experts, editor, proofreader and the materials production staff.

The team's work begins at the planning stage. The role of the team is to:

- identify the educational needs of the programme and decide how they will be met
- identify the learners' needs, describe characteristics and how they will affect the programme
- define both the general and specific objectives of the programme
- identify the available resources and constraints
- identify the media to be used
- outline the plans of the programme, which includes the:
  - delivery to be used, whether video, audio, video conferencing, Internet, print or face-to-face,
  - duration of the programme
  - number of learners to be enrolled
  - administrative structure of the programme
  - methods of collecting feedback information and how it will be used
  - budget for the course
  - course operation, for example, will the course have face-to-face tutorials?
  - tutor for the course.

Instructional designers must be able to work well with all team members no matter how trying the circumstances.

The role of the instructional designer

The role of the course developer, who is usually an instructional designer, in course planning and development is partly educational and partly administrative. Very often the subject specialists – who are contracted on a part-time basis – have very little knowledge of distance learning.

The instructional designer must work with the subject matter experts to determine the 'effectiveness' of the materials produced.

The functions of an instructional designer include:

- finding and briefing the materials writers
- designing the course
- working with writers to improve the quality of their materials and ensuring the course materials are educationally valid and that the language and instructions are clear
- preparing a production schedule
- preparing materials for print and checking that they are clearly linked with other course components
- structuring the text and checking details so that it is ready for printing
- arranging for the field testing of the course
- controlling the process of course development.

Development model

When designing distance education materials you should develop a model for the development of your learning materials. This model should include curriculum documentation, the design and production tasks, implementation and an evaluation and validation methodology (see Figure 2.1).

The model will differ depending on the type of course you are developing, but you must ensure that each part of the course goes through the same development process.

Before you finalize the model you should start to complete your course information document (CID) as outlined in *Planning a Course*, Chapter 2. Although at this stage you will not be able to complete the entire document it will give you an idea of the scope of the project.

Learner profile

The first step in developing your learning materials is to develop your course documentation. If you are developing a new course you should develop a learner profile and subprofile starting with a profile session as outlined in *Planning a Course* Chapters 4 and 5. The learner profile should be validated before the sub-profile is developed otherwise you may find that your learner profile has inaccuracies.

You should not try to complete the learner profile and the sub-profile in one session.

Figure 2.1 *Model for developing distance education learning materials*

The validated learner and sub-profile is the basis of your course documentation and without it, it is very difficult to produce relevant and effective learning materials.

Developing performance objectives

Once the learner profile is developed then the goals of the course, along with the general and specific objectives can be determined.

While the goals and general objectives do not necessarily have to be written in strict performance terms as outlined in *Planning a Course*, Chapter 6 it is essential that the objectives are measurable and describe the performance of the learners.

What is a performance objective?

Performance objectives are clear and precise statements of single meaningful units of learner behaviour. An objective should be written in performance terms, that is they must have a performance, condition and standard component. Performance objectives for the learners mean they have a clear idea of what they have to achieve. For the instructional designer and the subject matter experts, objectives allow them to select the appropriate content, use the most effective delivery methods and determine an appropriate evaluation.

Course design

Materials for distance education should be modular in design. A module is a major component of work or a topic to be delivered. Each module should be made up of individual units or topics that are smaller than modules but still are self-contained elements of work (see Figure 2.2).

Each module should have an introduction which explains how it relates to the other modules.

When you are designing your materials for distance education make them modular in design.

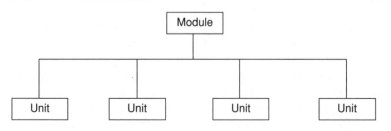

Figure 2.2 *Module design*

Unit design

The writers actually writing the individual units of work will need some form of template to help them structure their writing. While each unit may be on a different topic it is important that they have a consistent structure. The structure of the individual units is usually designed by the instructional designer. A unit can be made up of the following components:

- objectives
- introduction
- body content
  - reading
  - self-help questions
  - photographs
  - diagrams
  - graphs
  - flowcharts
- summary
- review (self help) test and answers
- other resources
- assignment

Objectives specify what material learners must know at the end of the unit in performance terms. Usually, there will be a general objective statement and a number of specific objectives, which detail exactly what the learners have to achieve.

The **introduction** gives the learner an overview of the content and explains why it is necessary to study the materials.

The **body content** is the text that includes photographs, diagrams, graphs and flow charts. There should also be self-help questions that test the learners' knowledge of the section they have just read. The **summary** is placed at the end of the body content and summarizes the main points of the unit.

The **self evaluation test** examines the learners' comprehension of the unit using various test items. This test is for self review, so answers should be provided.

Other resources that the learners will find useful include textbooks, videos, CD ROMs, video disks and Internet URLs. Other resources should provide additional information on the unit, but may not be essential to the study of the unit as these resources may not be available to all the learners.

An **assignment** may form part of the learners' overall assessment. Here learners are expected to apply what they have learned in the unit to a new situation. Typically the assignment would be marked by the tutor.

An alternative unit design could be as shown in Figure 2.5.

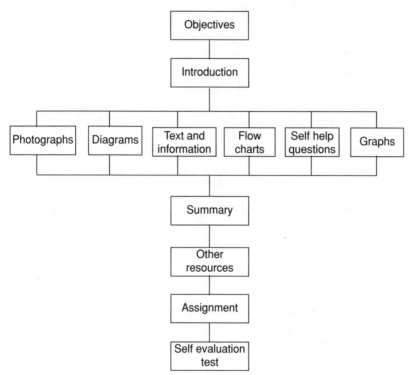

Figure 2.3   *Unit design*

PLANNING TO WRITE THE UNIT OF WORK

Since the unit objectives have been developed in the profiling session the subject matter expert will know what material is to be included, but they often find it difficult to know where to start.

Use the points below to help structure the unit of work.

- Plan the content page first
- Logically plan your paragraphs
- Give explanations and examples to expand your material
- Plan the complete unit of work before you begin writing

Develop a template for the writers to follow; they will appreciate it and the materials you receive will be better for it.

- Ensure all of the units' objectives are covered
- Ensure that material has been covered that enables the learners to complete their self-test and assignments
- Sequence the work carefully, from:
  - known to the unknown
  - concrete to the abstract
  - observation to reasoning
  - whole to the detailed view
  - explaining first things first, that is, following the correct chronological order
  - use well-known analogies, similes and metaphors where possible.
- Plan the unit so it does not overlap with other units of work
- Keep the target audience constantly in mind
- Write at a level learners will understand
- Keep the learners' workload at a constant but reasonable level when writing self-help questions and assignments.

The **introduction** should describe the topic you are discussing in general terms. It should also explain why it is useful or necessary to learn the topic. You should try to relate the present topic to similar topics with which the learners have had experience. The introduction should be motivational and make the learners want to read and complete all the exercises.

The **body content** is the text component of the unit and the main material from which the students will learn. The body content should include illustrations, photographs, flowcharts, graphs, tables and other visuals.

When developing the body content try to write user friendly text. It is important that you include access devices in your materials. Access devices make the text more accessible or 'user friendly' to the learners. Examples of access devices are content pages, visual sign posts, advanced organizers, objectives, introductions, overviews, headings, summaries, glossaries and subject indices.

Illustrations are often used in distance learning materials and form a significant part of the message in any written learning materials. Illustrations are used to:

- communicate more effectively with the learners
- present facts and figures in a different way
- emphasize certain points
- show relationships and ideas

- act as a visual 'shorthand'
- stimulate learners by varying the presentation
- help learners remember things
- be an activity for the learners
- show verbal concepts in a visual form
- show the internal working of objects.

Effective illustrations are:

- efficient in the way they present the information
- simple with no superfluous details
- easy to read and have clear labels
- present an unambiguous message
- able to be viewed clearly ie the correct size
- appropriate to the message being delivered, for example, a diagram, chart, map, schematic, time line, pictogram or cartoon.

Illustrations can be used to replace paragraphs of text and enable the learners to remember information clearly.

Photographs can also be part of your distance learning materials. The advantages of photographs are that they:

- show the actual object
- save time compared with the time it takes to draw a complex illustration
- are relatively simple to incorporate into documents.

Remember the old saying that a picture is worth a thousand words.

The disadvantages of photographs are that they:

- can have too many superfluous details and become distracting.
- date quickly, especially when there are people involved. For example, the style of clothes and hair.
- make it difficult to see the internal working of objects.

Page layout

Text formatting

Using correctly formatted distance learning materials is a significant aid to learners studying, learning and interacting with them. All too often learners find a confusing jumble of text and graphics crammed into a space that leaves little or no room for note taking. Learners will find learning materials difficult to follow where topic titles and

Remember that good page format makes text easier to read, relates the text to the illustrations and facilitates rapid scanning by the learner.

chapter headers are difficult to pick out from the text and where the font is difficult to read and inappropriate for the materials being presented.

A poorly formatted page can suffer from a combination of problems. It could have the text both left and right justified (lined up on both sides of the page just like a novel). The title, if there is one, may be placed too close to the text and be hard to distinguish from other text on the page, the page may not have a header or a page number and any charts, diagrams and/or illustrations may be difficult for learners to use as they do not correspond to the accompanying text.

Better page layout; means making sure that text is well set out on the page and does not confuse the learners (see Figure 2.4).

Good text layout aids learners by:

Remember that research has shown that text that has only been justified on the left is much easier to read.

- making your text easier to read
- providing an obvious pattern to the material
- emphasizing what is important
- directing attention to key points
- separating blocks of information
- facilitating rapid scanning and retrieval of information
- providing space for the taking of notes.

Use the following guidelines when formatting your learning materials.

Make sure that you have two to three people review your materials format.

- Leave a lot of white space on the page to break up the density of your text and allow for note taking.
- Place charts, diagrams and/or illustrations as close as possible to the related word explanations.
- Use bullets instead of numbers for lists, except when the procedure must be performed in a specific order.
- Use short lists separated by headings.
- Use a bold face and/or italics for points you want to emphasize. But don't overdo it.
- Use boxes around text portions of special interest.
- Use Arabic rather than Roman numerals and try to avoid using numbers such as 1.9.7.3 as part of a topic heading.

Justifying text on the page

A great deal of discussion has been centred around the lining up of text on both the left and right hand side of the page. Research indicates that text justified both on the left and right cause the legibility of the text to be impaired and makes it far more difficult for some learners to read.

(a)   (b)

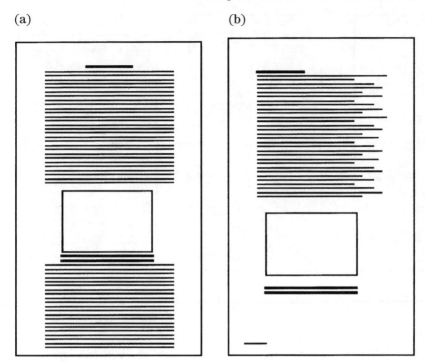

Figure 2.4   *Sample page format: (a) poor layout; (b) better layout*

Use of columns on the page

You may wish to consider a number of columnar formats for your layout. The most common, of course, is the single column. The single column is considered best for text materials that are continually being broken by tables, diagrams and graphs, provided that you space your paragraphs in the text by one or more lines. A two column format is useful if you are going to use icons as part of your text. However try not to place icons in your page margins as that tends to place the icon too close to the binding on the odd numbered page. A three column format is not recommended for straight-forward prose as the line lengths become too short. (see Figure 2.5)

Self-help questions

Self-help questions should be designed to keep the learners alert. Interaction with the material aids learning.

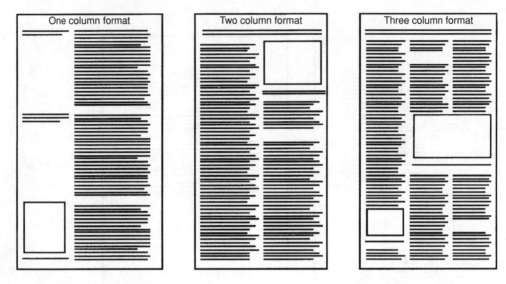

Figure 2.5   *Different column formats*

Every two to three pages of your learning materials, try to include a self-help question.

Self-help questions should follow the following guidelines.

- Self-help questions should be interesting, to encourage the learners to complete them.
- The questions should be motivational, for example: 'Let's see how many of these you can get right.'
- The questions should be helpful so they help clarify important points in the text.
- The questions should ask the learners to undertake a challenging task and motivate them to complete it. There should be a very good chance that the learners can be successful at answering the question so that they do not become discouraged.
- Questions should not be used for the simple recall of information. They should ask the learners to apply the information they have learned.
- The questions should be self assessed so that the learners can determine their own progress. This means that learners can study the model answers or their learning materials for the answers.
- The type of question should be different to add variety for learners.
- The questions should be directly linked to the material objectives otherwise there is little use in the learner completing them.

- The questions should give some indication of the length of the answer required, for example: 'Spend a few moments writing a short paragraph as an answer to this question'.
- Questions should be designed so that the learners have an opportunity to apply the knowledge they have gained'.

Summary

The summary should be a brief description of the information in the unit. It should remind the learners of the most important points covered in the unit and consolidate the material within that unit in the context of the overall module/course.

Summaries can also be used as an interactive device. You can ask learners to summarize the learning material as an activity. You could assist them by providing a set of headings under which they could complete the task.

Consider having learners summarize the learning materials as part of an interactive activity.

Assignments

Assignments are where learners apply the knowledge they have gained. As the assignment is often part of the overall assessment, it requires careful consideration and planning to make sure it meets the needs of the learners. The learners should be able to apply the knowledge gained to new situations.

Consider the nature of the assignment by asking yourself the following questions:

- Does it acquaint learners with an issue, concept or principle?
- Does it question learners' attitudes?
- Does it attempt to develop learners' ability to gather, collate and express ideas?
- Does it help develop skills?
- Is the assignment designed to help learners prepare for a formal examination?
- Is the main point of the assignment to give the learners feedback on their work?

The answers to these questions will help you to determine the form of the assignment. For instance, you should be able to determine if you should test the objectives individually or collectively.

Testing the objectives

In designing the assignment you first must decide how you are going to test the objectives. The assignment may take the form of:

- a definition
- an explanation
- an argument
- a comparison
- an analysis
- a activity or task
- a summary.

When you have determined how you will test the objectives, you can choose one or more of the following means of testing:

- discussion/essay
- review/summary
- project
- report
- practical work
- completion of diagram(s)
- short answers
- practice exam questions.

Testing the assignment

After you have set the assignment ask yourself the following questions to determine if the assignment is effective.

- Is the assignment clear and unambiguous?
- Have the learners been adequately prepared for the assignment?
- Has the educational background and the experiences of the learners been taken into account to determine if the assignment is suitable?
- How long will it take the learners to complete the assignments? (The best way to test this is to complete it yourself.)
- Can you prepare a model answer and a marking scheme for your assignment?
- Is there more than one way of answering the assignment?

Self-test

Self-test questions help the learners review the material, and break it up into manageable chunks. The test items should be directly related to the unit's objectives and should be similar to the type of test items included in any formal assessment.

FIELD TRIAL

It is essential that the learning materials be reviewed before they are fully implemented as a formal course. Here materials should be reviewed by subject matter experts to determine if they are technically correct before the field trial takes place.

The learning materials should be field tested with learners trial to help identify problems. The field trial can be evaluated using learner questionnaires and interviews together with tutor interviews.

CONCLUSION

Developing distance learning materials follows the same principles as other learning materials. However, in many cases the distance learners will only have the materials themselves to learn from. Therefore, the materials need to be carefully designed so that they encourage interaction.

Chapter 3
Preparing Teaching Materials for Your Use

SUMMARY

Preparing your own teaching and learning materials could end up being a complex task. Therefore, keep it simple (KIS) is the rule. The preparation of these materials should not eat into your time. The use of appropriate technology is encouraged. However, the materials you prepare are to assist in the teaching and learning process – they should not confuse or, worse, cause the learner to focus on the technology rather than the message. This chapter deals with the issues involved in preparing teaching and learning materials for use by you and your learners for a course that is already developed.

INTRODUCTION

As a learner, were you ever in a class where the teacher fumbled with the technology, even a simple overhead, while those around you became bored and restless? This is one example of technology getting in the way of teaching. But there are even worse problems when complex technology is used when simple technology would have been as effective.

On the other hand, isn't it great when you see someone 'do' a good presentation? Maybe they use 'flashy' overheads or a good video. Perhaps you could do that with access to the right equipment. The underlying notion of KIS of KISS (keep it simple, stupid) needs to be considered when you are preparing instructional material or the aids to help you teach or your learners to learn.

In this chapter the focus is on preparing materials that you want to develop to assist you in your teaching task. These could be various types of print materials, audio-visual materials or computer-based or computer-related materials. For the moment let us consider that these are technologies to be used as means of delivery of content, to provide information and some working space for the learners. These materials might be supplementary to existing course materials. (The issues of access and equity that the use of some of these technologies causes are discussed in Chapter 7.)

If all you do is tell, then the course content and the majority of the information is quickly forgotten. If learners see what is being discussed, the retention rate of the information improves. However, if learners have a chance to work with the new information, retention is even greater. So, remember that while you are preparing the material for you to use, you should also be preparing materials for the learners.

This chapter is in four parts:

Learners remember only about 10 per cent of what you tell them, but they will remember about 90 per cent of whatever it is, if you get them to practice.

- Where do you start?
- What is going to help you teach?
- Relating this to something for the learners
- Conclusion.

The next chapter discusses issues arising when you prepare materials for other teachers to use.

Chapter 5 discusses criteria for selecting appropriate existing course support materials, and Chapter 6 looks at developing materials for a 'new course' starting with a 'clean slate'.

WHERE DO YOU START?

In any consideration of preparing teaching and learning materials for your personal use, you must have a good grasp of what you are to teach and for what purpose. This means that your curriculum documents are the first source of guidance. The gathering of information from subject matter experts, Course Information Documents and associated forms, and the compilation of course documents is discussed in a companion volume, *Planning a Course*. Briefly, you will need to consider what print, audio-visual or computer-based information might aid your teaching and aid the learners' learning. Sometimes these may be provided or suggested but you may want to develop your own to best meet the needs of your learners.

WHAT IS GOING TO HELP YOU TEACH?

The first set of considerations involve *what you want to do:*

- pass on information
- show examples or illustrations of the new information and how it works
- give the learners second-hand experience by working through examples of the information in practice
- place the learners in hands-on situations and require them to demonstrate their abilities with the new information.

You will invariably want to do all of these things. But you are seeking to clarify the type of activities you could carry out and aids you would require for these activities. Table 3.1 sets out some of the types of activities you might want to conduct, a possible methodology, types of materials you might use and the types of linked materials for the learners (in italics).

The second set of considerations involve *the use of technology.* You have to decide:

- what in the content needs direct instructional materials support
- what in the instructional materials and content needs support through technology and what difficulties this could cause you
- what are the difficulties that the use of technology might cause to learners?
- what effect the use of any technology may have in detracting or deflecting concentration from the content. In other words, what will the students remember... will it be the information in the presentation, your presentation, or the particular technology that was used?

The second set of considerations involve what you might want the learners to do with the teaching materials. This could include some of the following activities:

- demonstrate their use of the new information
- describe the new information in an appropriate context

The key is first to tell the learner something, then show them something and finally have them practise whatever it is that you want them to learn.

Table 3.1   *Activities, methods and aids for teachers and learners*

Type of Activity	Possible Methodology	Possible Aids for Teacher *and Learner*
Pass on information	Lecture or class presentation	Overheads Handouts *Skeletal notes*
	Workbooks	*Workbooks*
	Research exercise	*Task outline with expectations and deadlines*
Show examples or illustrations of the new information and how it works	Worked examples	*Example sheets or workbook*
	Visual (and audio) presentation	Posters Slides Audio tapes
	Video presentation	Handout *Worksheet*
Give the learners experience by working through an example of the information at work	Tutorial Small group discussion	Notes
	Simulation	Briefing notes *Worksheets and briefing notes* *Access to computer-based simulation*
Place the learners in hands-on situations and require them to demonstrate their abilities with the new information.	Workshop	Handouts Notes Plans
	Simulation or role play	*Briefing notes*

- comment on the new information in an unfamiliar context
- use their skills and knowledge to demonstrate their ability to adapt to applying the new to 'novel' situations.

In working through these considerations, you will confirm the support materials that you need for the learners and a list of materials you require for your teaching.

You are now in possession of information about the resources you require. You will need to consider if these resources already exist or if you will have to develop and produce them. If there is existing print, audio-visual or computerized material to support your teaching, you will have to determine if these fit into the time available for the course. Remember that the available time is not just for your presentation; you may have to allow time for some activity by the learners and feedback tasks from the learners. In later chapters we discuss selection criteria for existing materials.

A third set of considerations involve *time and cost*. If you are faced with the task of preparing materials for your 'class', some of the considerations you will need to take into account are:

- the time you have available to you to prepare these materials; in other words, when they are needed
- the resources you have available to you
- the costs of preparing and producing this material.

In Table 3.2 several of the more common teaching and learning materials are set out against the activities and costs associated with the production of these materials and the demands on your time.

A fourth set of considerations involve *maintaining the integrity of the course*. In many courses the outcomes for the learners are collated against the outcomes of other learners within the institution or across institutions. This could be for entry-level considerations or some state or national certification. In this setting, the use of individual materials needs to be considered against ignoring or modifying the materials supplied by the 'central authority'. In some cases you may be able to consult with the specialists in the subject area, the special interest teacher association (eg, the English Teachers Association or the Educational Research Association) or the authority overseeing the course. At the very least you must make sure that the material you develop is going to support the intentions of the course and benefit the learners.

Table 3.2   *Materials, activities and generic costs*

Material	Activities	Costs
Overheads	Plan sequence Clearly write out or type masters; if typed, photocopy	• The costs associated with your time in planning the lesson/lecture • Any costs associated with typing or photocopying • Cost of overheads
Notes	Plan content Type masters Duplicate	• Planning time • Typing costs and time • Duplication costs of time, paper and ink
Workbooks	Plan content Type masters Duplicate	• Planning time • Typing costs and time • Duplication costs of time, paper and ink
Video	Plan content and script Shoot Edit Prepare support materials such as notes to go with video	• Planning time and writing and checking content • If simple: time, cost of tape If complex: cost of crew talent and … Edit time • As with print, time, typing layout and printing costs
Computer simulation	Preparation Select application Script and enter materials Beta test Support materials	• Plan the simulation • Assemble the information • Write the simulation in a way that can be translated to computer • Develop the simulation • Test and evaluate the simulation • As with video, there may be costs of developing and producing support materials

SOME BOTTOM LINE KIS (KISS)

The KIS or (KISS) rules as applied to presentation materials you want
to prepare are as follows.

Overheads

The text should be in the form of outlines only, not full sentences. To help you do this, remember:

- having too many overheads means your presentation may be only telling, and telling learners has a limited impact on learning
- use overheads to organize your presentation
- if you have reasonable handwriting consider using overheads with an outline on them and leave space for you (or a scribe) to add notes as the session progresses. There is one big advantage: it allows you to more easily maintain eye contact, rather than turning to the chalkboard or whiteboard
- no more than six points on any one overhead
- no more than seven words to a point
- keep the size of the lettering large so it can be read from the back of the room
- if possible, get to the room early to set up the projector
- if possible, carry a replacement bulb for the projector, or check there is a replacement bulb in the projector. This is important if others use the same equipment. Even with the best intentions someone may not tell you, the service staff or the audio-visual technician that a bulb has blown – so be prepared.
- most people are familiar with the standard technique of revealing the points on the OHT rather than just putting the OHT on the platen. However, it is possible to use adhesive tape to allow you to 'build-up' a presentation, as shown in Figure 3.1.

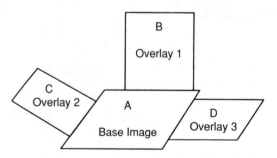

Figure 3.1   *Building-up a presentation with overlays*

Print

Designing notes for learners is a complex task. Not least is the balance to be struck between what you want to 'tell' the learners in the notes and the 'work' that the learners have to do with and on the notes. As a simple guide, the following points seem to work:

- keep the notes to a point form
- leave space on the notes or handouts for the learners to make notations
- consider using narrower columns of text as it can make reading easier for some readers.

Video

If you are preparing a video to support your presentations then you must consider the attention span of your audience, the depth of subject content you need to cover and the time and financial support available to produce your specific video.

Any video you plan to develop should be designed so that it can be used effectively with succeeding groups of learners. The amount of time and effort on your part in making the video should lead to time savings in other parts of your preparation. For example, a video tape of an experiment may not save you from doing the experiment. However, the video can be shown in advance so that learners know what to look for during the experiment. Then, after the experiment, the video can be shown to clarify any points. In this example the cost and time of making the video offsets the costs of setting up and repeating experiments.

The following points will help you in developing a video:

Typically, a person's attention span is about ten minutes or less. So in your video or computer based learning materials make sure that you keep the 'action' at a fairly high level and keep things moving along.

- in any one video, restrict the video to the point you want to make; avoid including points that are 'nice to know'.
- in any one video only present about five points as a maximum
- try not to extend the time in front of the screen beyond 20 minutes
- plan how to introduce and follow-up material in the video.

Material requiring computers

Currently many people are working on applications that can be used on personal or network computers. The problem of different and competing computer 'platforms' is disappearing as the major hardware and software developers move towards a common set of operating protocols.

At the same time, there is much hype about the possibilities of computers and the computer 'Superhighway' and the 'Internet'. The question of how they are to be used for education and training is largely ignored at the moment, because what the Internet offers is access to information for researchers for their teaching, but this is changing rapidly. This access to information via the Internet (and the nodes associated with it) offers the potential for learners to make enquiries of the available databases and for the learners to develop their own expertise. The implications of this for teachers and for learners are being worked through in practice and reported in the literature. With this taste of the future it is important to consider the underlying features that will be part of that future.

One of the first considerations with the use of computers is to make sure that computers are available and suitable for the use you intend. There have been cases of teachers developing material on their computers at home while the computers that the students would use did not have the memory to run the application, or the monitors were monochrome when the presentation was designed for colour. There are many variations on why computer incompatibility exists; be aware of it and determine before you start if you are going to have problems.

Also remember that not all people are comfortable with computers. No matter what the computer enthusiasts would like to believe, there are people of all ages and both sexes who prefer to gain information, education and training in ways other than by computer. If your intention to use computer-based instruction or testing would be a new initiative in your educational community, you must discuss your intentions with that community.

Some of the key elements in developing computer applications are as follows.

Try to test several applications before you start development. Not many of them are easy to use the first time, so you may have to allow some lead time to become familiar with an application. Then again, although an application seems easy, it may not have some of the features you need.

Thoroughly plan the process you want the learners to 'experience'. The big danger is that you will plan something for learners to 'work through', and all you will end up with is 'electronic page-turning', without the advantage of skimming or re-reading parts of the material that some learners seem to like and which is available to them in hard-copy texts. If you think of the process as one you want the learners to

If you are considering moving toward computer-based learning materials, you may want to consider conducting a learning styles inventory of your learners to help you determine if computer based learning is the right choice.

experience, then it is possible that you will consider the outcomes you expect from the learners at the end of the experience. To avoid the impression of electronic page-turning, use a base screen and have material added and subtracted, as in the overhead transparency overlays described above.

Be consistent in the way the learner is expected to interact with the computer. If you start out using a mouse to progress, don't switch to key strokes at some point. However, sometimes keystrokes, such as entering answers, are a natural means of progression from one part of the computer material to the next.

Try to develop time away from the screen. This serves two purposes: the first is to avoid eye strain, the second is that it allows others to use the computer. A simple strategy could be to print out random generated tests for learners to do away from the screen. While that is happening others can be going through other stages of material. One benefit of this is that fewer computers are needed.

The design of the actual screens should be kept simple. If the application you are using has a black and white option, design a screen in colour and then change it to black and white (or the grey scale). You may be surprised to see that the colours that stood out from one another are not so prominent in the grey scale. This is because some colours, translated to the grey scale (ranging from white, through various greys to black), have the same 'grey-scale value'. This may help you determine the colour components of your presentation screens.

Feedback to the learner during their interaction with your computer package is an issue you need to consider. Many of the applications used to develop computer-based material have in-built feedback responses such as noises; others allow text feedback. At issue is not that there is feedback but the style and form of that feedback. The real problem is that the feedback you devise is trying to second-guess the thinking of the learner when they make a wrong response. (A question to consider: is it correct to assume that when the learner makes a right response it is because the learner 'knows' what is right?)

Test what you have developed. Given that these are computer materials for you to use, this may sound a little silly because you will test them with your learners. But consider this: learners expect to be in contact with people who are experts on the subject and in the way the components of the subject are taught. There is a real question of professionalism when students are used as testers. The main problem is how you re-teach if the computer-based material did not produce the results you expected. You may have to decide on revamping and continuing, or abandoning the use of computers.

Keeping records of learning progress on computer is possible, which raises issues of security and the integrity of the information.

RELATING MATERIALS TO THE LEARNERS

Materials prepared to assist you to teach should also assist the learner to learn.

To present the material you will have worked out a sequence for the course or lesson. But you may still need to consider the following questions.

The first is to do with the time available for presentation of the course, the lesson or segment of the lesson. The second is that the educational and training effect of a computer-based presentation with video and audio clips will be minimal if all that the learners remember was that they were entertained, they used a computer and... nothing about the content. Third, this problem of technology 'skewing' the educational and training process is even more the case if the learners consider that they are only able to address this content, their learning, their training, through technology. In other words, their part in the learning process is as a passive recipient.

You will also need to consider the effect of using technology on your use of time for teaching and the learners' use of time for learning.

These considerations will focus you on what is needed to assist your teaching, what you need to prepare for learners, and what learners will require to assist them in their learning.

CONCLUSION

This chapter was started with the exhortation to 'keep it simple'. You need to balance this imperative with the complexity of the course content and the need to facilitate the learners in their task of learning.

If you are going to develop your own support material and use audio visual or computer-based materials, then you will need to consider the learners: are they able to demonstrate the input to their thinking or actions as a result of your presentation?

Chapter 4

Preparing Materials that Someone Else is Going to Teach

SUMMARY

Learning materials are often unfit for use because no systematic design methodology has been applied to their development process. Because of this institutions are calling for the development of learning materials that can be handed to anybody, from the beginning teacher to the expert, ready for delivery to the student. What do most of these materials tend to look like? How does the teacher sift through the morass, make sense of it all and make them their own? How are these types of materials put together in the first place?

This chapter will outline the strategies for developing teacher-independent materials, and getting them ready for delivery to the student.

INTRODUCTION

Do you remember the first day you walked into a school or similar institution to start work and were handed a 'set of notes' to 'teach'? Perhaps you were lucky in that you had taught the course before and the notes just added to the materials you already had on the subject. Or maybe it was your first teaching job and the notes weighed heavily in your hand and your first thought was, 'What do I do with this lot?'

Many of you will recognize this scene and perhaps agree that even for the most experience, being handed a set of 'notes' like this can be a daunting experience. Schools and institutions are slowly beginning to realize that handing a prospective teacher a set of notes is not the best way to introduce either the novice or the 'expert' to teaching. The practice can also be an expensive one as the 'learning curve' required by the teachers to familiarize themselves with the notes is often longer than anticipated and the end result less than expected. To make matters worse, as the weeks and months pass and you strive to make sense of the notes and make them the best they can be, they of course become yours, so the day you leave the school or institution for 'greener pastures' you take them with you, along with your knowledge and experience.

This chapter is directed to those of you given the task of preparing teacher-independent learning materials. The kinds of materials you are going to prepare might contain up-to-date course documentation that describes the rationale for the course, its goals and objectives and list of the topics the learner must learn. The materials might also include a teacher guidebook, readings, a list of usable learner activities and a number of skeletal lesson plans that can be personalized by the teacher and used to develop a delivery strategy appropriate to their own teaching style and the learners in their classroom.

TYPES OF TEACHER-INDEPENDENT MATERIALS: ADVANTAGES AND DISADVANTAGES

Use a script based approach when developing a learning guide when you need conformity and consistency in the message being delivered to the learner. For example, reviewing the goals and objectives of an organization.

Teacher-independent learning materials are often called 'blueprints'. This is somewhat of a misnomer. Plans or blueprints for a house, for example, indicate in great detail the size and shape of all the pieces that will be needed if the house is to meet specifications. To some, the use of the term 'blueprint' when applied to learning materials also indicates that all of the pieces that will be needed for the teacher to deliver those materials to the learners have been put in place – and this is not necessarily the case.

How the materials are developed depends upon the range of abilities expected of the teacher in the classroom and the learner who is going to use them to learn. For example, some blueprints are designed and written in a script format. These often include, in fine detail, not only the words the teacher will say to the learners but directions to the spot upon which they should stand in the classroom. At the other end of the scale, materials are often designed with little or no detail at all, listing only a few basic aims and objectives and omitting any discussion of delivery methodology or what the teacher must pass on to the learner.

Both of these extremes have their advantages and disadvantages and prior to starting to prepare any materials, you will have to determine what approach you are going to follow and what elements are going to be included in the final package. Table 4.1 outlines the advantages and disadvantages of the two extremes and a so-called middle-of-the-road approach.

Table 4.1 *Advantages and disadvantages of the three possible approaches to the development of teacher-independent learning materials*

	Advantages	**Disadvantages**
Script approach	• consistency in teaching approach/methodology • para-professional staff could be used	• teacher not able to personalize • no ownership of materials by the teacher • difficult to add new materials • motivation to learn could be low • can be expensive for the institution to produce and maintain
Middle-of-the road approach	• overall consistency in teaching approach • materials can be personalized • some materials can be added if needed • motivation to learn could be average to high • could be maintained by the teacher	• can be expensive for the institution to produce • skilled teacher needed to make it work
Little or no detail approach	• materials can be personalized and owned • other materials can be easily added • motivation to teach could be high • motivation to learn could be high	• lack of consistency in teaching approach • can be over-personalized • skilled teacher needed to make it work • institution has little or not • control over materials • can be expensive for the institution to continue the practice

The following discussion will describe a middle-of-the-road approach to the development of teacher-independent materials. It is assumed that the materials you will be preparing have been based on a systematic approach to learning materials design and have useful documentation.

ITEMS THAT MAKE UP TEACHER-INDEPENDENT MATERIALS

Teacher independent learning materials should include all the necessary information for the learners, but make sure that you keep the materials as simple as possible.

Many items can be included as part of the teacher-independent learning materials package; at a minimum the package should include:

- course documentation
- course notes
- suggested readings
- learning event sheets plus basic lesson plans that include suggesting learning activities and delivery strategies.

Course documentation. This should include information about the course such as its rationale and basic aims and objectives and a list of the various topics the learner will be expected to learn as part of the course. This kind of information will help the teacher better understand how the materials should be presented to the learners.

Course notes. These can be materials given to the learner to supplement the text materials they have to use, or they can be materials used in place of a text(s).

Suggested readings, learner event sheets and skeletal lesson plans. These are often bound into a teacher guide or workbook. The readings can be materials that go beyond the course notes to help provide the teacher with a wider view and a context for the course as well as providing additional information that can be used as other learning materials are being presented. Learning event sheets in teacher-independent materials, if they are to be useful to all concerned, should be such that a teacher has to develop part of them as a lesson plan in order to make the event a viable learning experience.

PREPARING THE LEARNING EVENT SHEETS

The biggest problem that you will face when preparing middle-of-the-road teacher-independent materials is ensuring that you have provided enough information so the materials can be delivered but have not stifled the creativity needed to deliver those materials effectively. There has to be room in your design for the teacher to insert their ideas and thought but at the same time accept the delivery methodology and strategy that you have suggested and designed the event around. One of the ways this can be accomplished is to use a combination learning event sheet and a skeletal lesson plan format. Using this approach, you prepare the learning event sheet by listing all the various macro events using one or a number of delivery strategies, all within an overall time frame. These events are derived from the objective(s) determined for this portion of the course. At the same time you must also provide a lesson plan format into which the teacher has to develop, based on your delivery strategy, those things they know will make the learning event viable. You can also prepare the learning event sheet by suggesting alternative delivery methodologies. For example, as well as using a guided discussion with the group, a role play could be prepared based on a case study and a number of readings. The teacher could then use two methodologies to deliver the lesson.

Activity 1: Preparing an Oral Presentation

Purpose
This activity focuses on a discussion of the techniques used during cross-examination.

Objective
Upon completion of this activity, learners will be able to describe what is required of them during cross-examination and how to prepare for cross-examination and argument.

Time
1½ hours (8:30–10:00).

Process
The teacher will:
● Discuss appropriate hearing conduct
● Lead a guided discussion on the presentation of evidence and the types of evidence that are acceptable during a hearing
● Lead a guided discussion on cross-examination
● Demonstrate cross-examination techniques in a role play situation.

Materials
● Overhead projector
● *Responding to Cross-examination Guidelines.*

Figure 4.1   *Learning event sheet*

The example in Figure 4.1 shows a typical learning event sheet that you would design and prepare. There the learners are social workers being prepared to give evidence in court. The learning event sheet lists a number of separate guided discussion that take place in a time period of one and a half hours. How those discussions should take place and the details of the discussion are left to the teacher to determine and prepare.

The lesson plan shown in Figure 4.2 is an example of one that can be partly prepared by the teacher based on the learning event sheet. In this case each guided discussion would be broken down by the teacher into a series of smaller events appropriate to the teacher's personal style. Also listed is the introduction or overview and summary or conclusion. A skeletal plan could be prepared to accompany the learning event sheet. This plan might contain an introduction and conclusion portion and headings to indicate what portion of the lesson needs to be developed.

You should plan on developing one learner event sheet for every one of the stated topics shown on the profile for the course. Prior to your developing any learning events sheets, however, you will need to review the following general considerations with respect to making any choice regarding a delivery methodology:

- What are the needs of the learners during this learning event?
- What are the needs of the teachers during this learning event?
- Will the learners be at a simple knowledge level, an application level or a synthesis level? What is the best delivery method for them?
- How familiar with the delivery strategy will the person be who might be delivering these materials? If they are not that familiar with it, how and where can they practise?
- Will the teacher be willing to learn a new skill? Is there a chance the teacher may drop the suggested methodology in favour of something else and if they do, will it detract from the course?
- How well will the learners know the delivery methodology being considered? Are they going to be confused?
- What constraints might the teacher be facing with regard to lesson time, group size and both the learning and physical environment?
- What role will be expected of the learners and what role will they expect the teacher to play?

When you choose your delivery strategy take both the learners' and the actual (physical) environment into consideration. For example, don't set up a role play where the people may want to arrange chairs in a circle in a room with theatre style seating.

When preparing a learning event plan, consider the needs of the learner first. Next consider your own needs. Once this is done think about sequencing the topics.

Activity 1: Preparing an Oral Presentation

Objective
Upon completion of this activity, learners will be able to describe what is required of them during cross-examination and how to prepare for cross-examination and argument.

Time
1½ hours (8:30–10:00)

Time	Topic	Resources
	Introduction	
5 mins	● Answer any questions arising from the previous lesson ● Reference previous lesson (case study) and relate to preparing an oral presentation	
30 mins	**Giving evidence** ● Divide learners into small groups (six people) and have them determine the five most important things that must be observed by a social worker when giving evidence ● Have each group report back to the large group ● Review answers with the participants	Flip chart or whiteboard Guidebook notes
45 mins	**Cross-examination** ● Outline the purpose of cross-examination ● Outline the types of questions asked in cross-examination ● Outline the methods of cross-examination questions and the advantages and disadvantages of each ● Review errors made in cross-examination ● Hand out *Responding to Cross-examination Guidelines* and have learners place these guidelines in their workbooks ● Cross-examination role play. Teacher/learner using the *Questions for Cross-examination* sheet	Flip chart or whiteboard Guidebooks notes Handout sheet
10 mins	**Wrap-up** ● Answer any final questions arising from the lesson ● Set the stage for the next lesson	

Figure 4.2 *Typical lesson plan*

Once you have answered these questions to your satisfaction, your next task is to consider how you are going to sequence the topics of each lesson. Typically at the macro level the course topics have been arranged based on a number of issues. However, at a micro level you will have to consider one or more of the following approaches to the sequencing of the lesson topics.

Sequencing the various learning event topics

Chronological. Using the chronological approach, your topics would be arranged according to when various events occurred. A typical example here would be a history lesson.

Order of performance. Here topics are arranged in the order they are performed. A typical example here might be taking apart a machine or similar device where it is important for the learner to know the correct sequence of events. In some circumstances backward chaining can also be used with great success.

Known to the unknown. This approach asks you to consider what the learner already knows and build on its foundations. An example of this approach might be the learning of a new computer software program. Here the teacher could use prior knowledge of a relational database to introduce the new topic of spread sheets.

Taxonomic. This approach is common in science and engineering and has, of course, been used in education to classify educational objectives. A typical example might be the structure of organisms in biology.

Simple to complex. Here the topic is arranged to begin with the most simple concept or task and to progress to the more complex in a logical fashion until the topic has been covered. An example of this might be the very young child learning about the members of their immediate family and the relationship of each to the other, then moving upward and outward into the wider community as new topics are introduced. The simple to complex approach also has some of the element of the known to unknown approach.

There are a number of other approaches to sequencing learning events; however they are less appropriate to the development of teacher-independent learning materials.

One other consideration is the availability of resources to deliver the learning materials. You will need to establish what is available *now* in terms of instructional equipment and facilities and how and when they should be used. Do they have to be booked? Who will do this? Is the teacher expected to do it?

It is difficult, if not impossible, to forecast what instructional equipment and facilities will be available to the teacher in the future to deliver the learning materials, but it is important to give this issue some consideration. You must try to keep your technology options simple. One trap you should avoid is setting up a learning event that relies on some form of advanced technology and assuming that the resource will still be available at some unknown future date. For example, a video conference centre has just been installed in your institution and you have designed a lesson that calls for some teacher/learner interactivity using the facility. Can you be sure it will still be operational at some future date? A second error that can be made in this area is to assume that not only will the technology still be operational but that it has expanded to include the latest development, for example that the video conference system has been expanded to include some form of on-campus desktop video.

Sequencing each learning event topic

As well as sequencing your learning topics, each learning event must of course have its own internal sequence. It must have a sound beginning that contains an overview of what is to come. This overview should also motivate the learners to expand their energies in learning the topic at hand. The learning event also needs a middle, a place where the presentation portion of the lesson is made, and it must have an end where what has happened is all brought together for the learner.

The presentation portion of a learning event should contain three important elements. First, it should give the learner some new information. Second, the new information should be followed by examples of where it all fits in the overall scheme of things, and third, some provision should be made for the learner to practise the new skill. Using the previous example as a guide, the chosen delivery methodology for this learning event includes an introductory portion delivered by the teacher, followed by a guided discussion based on readings and the previous learning events. This is called the *tell* portion of the learning event that sets out what is to happen and then provides the new information.

The next part of the learning event is called the *show* portion. In this example this is carried out using a role play with the teacher in the role of the social worker giving evidence, helped out by learners who have been briefed beforehand. The learning event is concluded at this point with no opportunity for the learner to practise. The reason for this lies

The first thing you have to do is to get the attention of the learners, next you need to give them a 'hook' on which to hang their previous experiences, and once you have done that, they might be ready to learn something!

in the fact that the topic is too large to be carried out in the time available. Rather than cram a great deal of material into one learning event at the risk of seriously reducing the learning that could take place, the decision was made to make the practice session part of the next event.

Finally, a learning event needs an end – a place where the teacher presents a brief summary of what has happened, reminds learners of the relevance of this topic to other topics and sets the scene for the next event. In our example, because the decision was made to put the practice portion of the learning event into the next session, it is important that the teacher concludes by, first, providing follow-up materials to reinforce what has occurred and, second, preparing the learner for the next event by providing a description of what will happen and the role the learner will be expected to play.

The events of instruction

It is important that when you are designing and developing the learning event sheets you consider what has been termed the 'events of instruction' (Gagné, 1977). These are:

- gaining attention
- informing the learner of the objective
- stimulating recall of prerequisite learning
- presenting the stimulus method
- providing learning guidance
- eliciting the performance
- providing feedback about performance correctness
- assessing the performance
- enhancing retention and transfer.

Gaining attention. The most important step in any learning event is to focus the attention of the learner on the task at hand and trying to ensure that this attention is enough to sustain the interest of the learner throughout the learning event. Attention can be achieved through the use of an unusual or different event: the teacher doing something different in the classroom or, in the case of a multi-media presentation for example, some eye-catching sequence to grab the attention of the learner.

Informing the learner of the objective. The learner needs to be informed of what is going to happen during the learning event so they can focus on that event and sort out what is relevant and what is not. The teacher can do this by simply telling the learners, 'Today we will be covering...' or it can be presented to the learners using an overhead transparency.

Stimulating recall of prerequisite learning. So learners are able to put the new information into a context based on what they already know, it is important that the learning event contains something that causes them to recall a prior event, evaluate it and use it as the foundation on which the present event will build.

Presenting the stimulus material. When the new materials are presented it is important that the learner is told of the generalities of the operation linked to a context or background, along with the factors, knowledge and skill associated with what is to be learned. It is also important that attention is focused on the relevant parts of the instruction.

All of the above make up the *telling* portion of the learning event.

Providing learning guidance. One of the most important things a teacher can do for the learners is to provide them with a means of encoding the information. In providing learning guidance, a teacher might show the steps involved in carrying out a task or suggest how the learner can complete a task.

This is the *showing* portion of the event.

Eliciting the performance. This is the practice portion of the learning event, the part where learners are expected to respond to all that has gone on before and demonstrate their learning. It is important that this event is not confused with evaluation; learners here are all still learning, they are not being tested.

This is the *doing* portion of the event.

Providing feedback about performance correctness. In this part of the learning event, feedback is given to the learners so they can determine if they have performed correctly. If true learning is to take place, the learner has to be able to judge how well they have performed compared to some set criteria.

Assessing the performance. Performance assessment is concerned with learners demonstrating their total understanding of the topic. This is the *evaluation* portion of the learning event in which the teacher must devise a methodology to determine if the event has been successful and learning has taken place.

Enhancing retention and transfer. If the event has been successful, the learner will be able to transfer what they have learnt to other situations and use it in different ways. To help ensure that this happens in an appropriate manner, it is important that the teacher provide sufficient learning practice and sufficient feedback to the learner about their performance so adjustments can take place.

Checking your learning event sheets

A useful mnemonic that can be used in the development of specific learning events is ROPES. This can help you as the designer of the learning event sheet to ensure that all of the necessary element have been included and also served as a useful check as you review your designs.

> Before you do a final review of your material, develop a checklist of the things you will be presenting, things you will be evaluating and things you will be summarizing. Make sure that they are all part of your learning materials.

R – Review. Here you should provide a review of the previous topic so the learner can understand where the topic fits into the course.

O – Overview. An overview of what is to come should be provided as a form of advanced organizer for the learners.

P – Presentation. This is where new materials are presented to the learner and contain the three elements: *telling* the learners what it's all about; *showing* them how it's done; and having them *practise* the new skill.

E – Evaluation. This is where the new skill as practised by the learner is checked for errors.

S – Summary. This is where the teacher makes a concluding statement and gets the learners ready for the next learning event.

Final considerations

The final considerations that should be made with regard to the design and development of teacher-independent learning material relate to how the person delivering the materials is going to do so when someone else has designed and developed the materials. To a certain extent this is one of the reasons for the development of course documentation, but in many cases teacher-independent materials need one more piece of information regarding the infrastructure required to support the course. This support is often taken for granted by teachers who develop their own materials but it is vital to the success of the course. The considerations here include information regarding facility requirements and the layout of that facility needed for the materials to be successfully delivered to the learners; and information regarding any audio-visual equipment requirements and the learning materials that have to be passed on to the learner. If a system to support the course is not put in place, no matter how well developed the course documentation, course notes, readings and learning activities are, the course will, in all probability, fail. An example of a typical document needed to support the course is shown in Figure 4.3.

CONCLUSION

This chapter has outlined the various considerations that need to be made prior to the design and development of teacher-independent learning materials. It is very important that when you are involved in this kind of project you make sure that the materials being developed are structured so the teacher is able to 'inject' his or her personality and style into the materials to ensure that they are delivered in a manner appropriate to the learning environment. This is not easy and will require the course materials to have good documentation that includes measureable objectives from which delivery strategies can be developed. Given the nature of some learning materials and the possible learning environment, it may be necessary for you to make a number of delivery suggestions with their own learning event sheets so that the teacher can use that which is most appropriate.

Finally, remember that you should keep your delivery strategies as simple as possible and not rely on advanced technology that may create a barrier between the teacher and the materials they have to deliver.

COURSE SUPPORT DOCUMENT

COURSE IDENTIFICATION

Course coordinator: _____

Course title: _____

Course length: _____ Time: _____ to _____

Number of learners: _____ minimum _____ maximum

Course date: _____ Location: _____ Room no. _____

Teacher: _____ Co-teacher: _____

FACILITY REQUIREMENTS

Classrooms (no.):_____ Break-off rooms (no.): _____

Special rooms (no.): _____ Describe: _____

FACILITY LAYOUT

Conference ☐   Theatre ☐   Circle ☐   U-shape ☐

Classroom: Tables joined ☐   Tables open ☐   Herring-bone ☐

Banquet: Round tables ☐   Square tables (back-to-back) ☐

AUDIO-VISUAL EQUIPMENT REQUIREMENTS

Flip charts ☐   no. ___   VCR/VTP ☐   VHS ☐   Beta ☐

TV monitor ☐   no. ___   size ___   Overhead projector ☐

Slide projector ☐   Film, slide, overhead projector screen ☐

Cassette deck ☐   Other: _____

MATERIALS REQUIREMENTS

Flip chart pads ☐   no. ___   Writing paper pads ☐ no. _____

Graph paper pads ☐   no. ___   Masking tape ☐ amt. _____

Flip chart pads ☐   no. ___   Flip chart markers ☐

OHP markers ☐   Writing markers ☐

Name tags ☐   Name tents ☐

Videotape(s):   Yes ☐ (attach list)   No ☐

Film(s):   Yes ☐ (attach list)   No ☐

Text(s):   Yes ☐ (attach list)   No ☐

Overheads: Yes ☐ (attach list)   No ☐

Handout material: Yes ☐ (attach list)   No ☐

Handout material to be: Loose ☐   Stapled ☐   Three-hole punched ☐

In three-ring binders ☐   Other: _____

Tests: Yes ☐ (attach list)   No ☐

Pre-course material: Yes ☐ (attach list)   No ☐

Post-course material: Yes ☐ (attach list)   No ☐

Other: Yes ☐ (attach list)   No ☐

ATTACHMENTS

Film(s):   Yes ☐   No ☐

List attachments:

_____

_____

_____

SPECIAL INSTRUCTIONS/COMMENTS

_____

_____

_____

Figure 4.3   *Course support document*

Chapter 5

Criteria for Selecting Prepared Instructional Materials

SUMMARY

The education and training world is a comfortable place to live and work in when the resources you require can be picked off the shelf as needed.

However, off-the-shelf materials can be a problem for someone new to selecting prepared course materials. They have to determine the criteria they should use in justifying the selection (or rejection) of prepared material. This chapter explains a systematic approach to appraising the suitability or otherwise of this material. The criteria are based on the needs of instruction, of the teachers and of the learners.

INTRODUCTION

Many teachers face the task of making decisions about selecting audio-visual and other materials, such as textbooks, for use in teaching. This task is made more difficult by the need to select from a sometimes vast and bewildering array of prepared materials. Without a set of uniform guidelines to enable a sensible comparison between materials, the task of appraising these materials and coming to a conclusion can be nigh impossible.

What follows is a set of steps to assist you in the task of appraising already existing materials to determine if they could be appropriate for supporting the course. It is assumed that you would do this appraising with a team; in some situations this may not be the case. However, even if carried out by an individual, the steps outlined here will assist in the systematic appraisal of materials.

Organization of the chapter

Consider developing a guide to help you rate the content of the learning materials.

This chapter is in two parts. The first, The Basic Considerations, assumes that you have collected (or will collect) a variety of existing materials that might be appropriate for a particular course. It outlines the preliminary steps in collating the information needed to provide a fair and equitable comparison between material.

The second, The Steps in Resource Appraisal, works through a set of steps you could take and the criteria you could use when you determine the suitability of this material for your course. Towards the end of the chapter is a diagram representing the steps, which could be used as a basis for developing a pro-forma to help you in appraising existing material.

THE BASIC CONSIDERATIONS

You must have firmly established the course criteria you are trying to satisfy. These should be on paper and available to any other people involved in the process. If you have Course Information Documentation (CID), this will provide that information. Use the CID documents to determine the needs. Clues to this could be found in the objectives of the course or statements derived from course objectives. They need to be agreed by the people taking part in the appraisal.

If you or your team members feel unsure about judging good or bad material or the lack of criteria for suitability, then the steps in appraising material described here should help; they have helped others.

There are three questions that need to be answered before setting about resource appraisal.

1. What resources material to support this teaching and learning already exists?

The first task is find out about the availability of materials from various sources; these could be libraries or distributors who hire or sell materials. The product available from these sources should be evaluated and, if usable and within your budget, bought and used.

2. What appropriate material already exists in the organization where you are working?

Before you spend any money on existing resources, make sure you have searched extensively for relevant materials that already exist in your organization and check whether your organization has access to this material through other resource centres. It's all too easy to over-look possibilities close to home.

3. What happens if you find nothing exists 'out there' or within your organization?

Often course support materials don't exist in a form that is convenient. The question then arises about making material. While this will be dealt with in the next chapter, let there be a word (or two) of warning here. Frequently inexperienced people assume that making a resource such as a video or a set of notes is easy. This is not necessarily so. Even in times of tight budgets it may be easier and more cost efficient to buy appropriate pre-produced learning material to support your course, rather than undertake the task of producing your own (see Chapter 6).

THE STEPS IN RESOURCE APPRAISAL

If you have Course Information Documentation this will indicate the objectives agreed to and noted. These will serve as a guide and focus to the content in the material under review. Having determined the objec-tives it is then appropriate to work systematically through your assem-bled materials and appraise them.

Most forms of media can be evaluated using six basic criteria: objectives, presentation, information, content, level and effectiveness.

To assist you and/or the members of the group working with you on the appraisal, you might consider developing a pro-forma. This could be based on the scheme outlined in Figure 4.1 at the end of the chapter, or you could devise your own – the use of a pro-forma is only to provide the person(s) collating the information with a common format.

Step 1: Identifying the resource or pre-produced course material

Note the title or any identifying feature of the material. This will help as a reference in later discussion, particularly if there is a lot of material being reviewed. If it is a film or videotape you should note such things as format, as this may affect the technical suitability for use with equipment already in your organization. In all cases note where possible the date of production of the material as this may give an indication of the 'life' of the resource.

For example, if you are appraising material that includes visuals of people, features such as hair-styles or clothes can distract today's learners from the messages in the visual prepared for learners of five to eight years ago. If you are expecting this new course and the support material to have a self-life of five years, then at the end of that period these images could be a decade or more out of date.

Step 2: Relating the content of the resource of the needs of the course

Using the established objectives, read, view, and discuss the material in an orderly manner. While doing this, consider the needs that you have established and ask yourself if this support material will satisfy these needs. This will enable you to check if the material needs some or all of the objectives of the course. It is unlikely that any material will fully meet these needs, so note down those objectives or criteria that the material does satisfy.

If the material seems to satisfy some or all of the objectives then perhaps this could be suitable course support material. However, you should not assume that other criteria will be satisfied as well. This assumption is tested in the next set of steps.

Step 3: Determine the appropriateness of the sequencing and pace in the material

In the teaching and learning setting, the sequence and pace of presentation of information are important considerations. If you have found some material that might contribute to the teaching and learning, then you should check that the sequencing and pace is appropriate.

Sequencing

The form of presentation of the material must have an internal logic and a sequence that does not cause confusion to the learner. This logic should also conform to *your* logic of presentation of the course. In other words, your presentation sequence and the sequence of presentation in this support material should not conflict.

If the structure or sequence of the material is not clear or could lead to confusion then you should consider discarding the material. However, it might be possible to remedy the situation if the use of an introduction or some other strategy overcomes the problems. For example, in the use of text, and with appropriate copyright undertakings, it might be possible to use the informative section of a chapter. With videotape, it could mean playing only the appropriate parts of the tape.

If these remedies are not feasible, you should conclude that this material is not suitable. When this decision is made, you must make a note that the material was inappropriate for the purpose. If need be you should get the people you are working with to 'sign off' this material. It saves time through stopping people going over the same materials at later appraisal sessions.

Pace

If the sequence and the structure are suitable, then you need to give some consideration to the pacing of the presentation of the content in each sequence. The pace of presentation may be either too slow or too fast and will affect the way in which the learners react to the material. Judging pace of presentation is difficult; however, as a rule of thumb, there is a pacing problem with the material if you find your interest waning, or from your background knowledge you find yourself wanting to add information. You also have to take into account the fact that learners react to instructional material in different ways, so you need to make sure that there is clarity in the instructional materials used.

Some possible problems and strategies to overcome them

In video presentations, for example, if there are parts which are having pacing problems then strategies may need to be developed to reduce this effect. Sequences that are too fast may be replayed. Sequences that are too slow could be dealt with by asking the learners to note down information in the sequence – this has them being active taking notes during the slow section of the video.

With print materials the problems of structure and sequence may be overcome by developing a reading guide so that the learners are advised which sections to read and in what order. The problems with pace in print material may have more to do with the learners' ability to cope with the language and the writer's style than the content.

Step 4: Judging how up-to-date the content is

As you have now worked through the material you are reviewing, you should be ready to judge whether the material is up-to-date. In other words, is the content of the material relevant to the needs of the course, your teaching and the work of the learners?

If the material is not current then you may wish to consider if the out-of-date material has some historical significance. This is a danger point: if the historical material would be 'nice to know' and you decide to use the material, you may be cluttering up the learning. In this case it may be wiser to discard the material. If, however, the historical material can be classified as 'need to know', then you must consider strategies to incorporate the material into the presentation of the course. If it has no redeeming features, you and your colleagues should 'sign off' the material.

Step 5: Assessing for comprehension

You next need to determine if the material is at a level of comprehension suitable for the learners. Should you consider that the level of comprehension is too low or too high, then a decision needs to be made about a possible strategy to make the material appropriate. If you and your colleagues consider the material to be too low, then the most probable decision is to reject it. If the level of comprehension is too high, then one strategy is to consider introductory activities and including these as the need for prior knowledge. This will result in more work. The need to develop activities and incorporate this 'advanced' material may be time-consuming and has the potential to divert learners, because it is only natural that learners will focus on areas they see their teachers featuring.

Step 6: The good, the bad and the outright dangerous

The material might have survived your evaluation so far. However, there are some further aspects you need to take into account. While many materials have good points, sometimes the inclusion of misinformation may make their use questionable. The definition of 'misinformation' is up to you; however, teachers do recognize misinformation or bad practice when it surfaces. The reason for this is simple: their experience shows that the biggest danger in showing bad examples in material is that some learners mistake this for a good example. This is particularly important when showing or discussing safety matters.

Where safety is concerned, most educators and trainers recommend that you only use materials that show the correct procedure. If the material shows bad or misinformation among good information, you may consider strategies to exclude the misinformation, but the energy you will have to expend to do this may outweigh any advantage in using the 'good bits'. Therefore it is probably in your interest to put this problem-ridden material aside. Make sure it is signed off by all of you.

How far have you progressed?

By now you will have eliminated material because:

● it did not meet your objectives
● the structure, sequence and/or pace were not appropriate
● the content or the level of comprehension was not suitable or the material contained misinformation.

What next?

In most appraisal processes two situations arise. The first and most common is that all the materials are rejected as unsuitable. When you reach this moment, you might consider this process to be a waste of time – and you would be wrong. You now have a considered opinion that the available material is unsuitable for your course. With this information on the unsuitability of 'all' available materials, you have just developed the best case to support your claim for the need to produce new material. In the second situation, there are two piles of material left on the table; sometimes there are three. The first pile is the rejects; the second is the 'could use' pile; and if there is a third pile, it is of suitable material.

Now you and the people working with you have to be very firm. The reject pile should be rejected. Sometimes you have to let others know your response to the material; this letter or phone call may require tact.

Then you face the problem of how to incorporate the 'could use' material. Here again it pays to be ruthless. However you need not behave without mercy. Sometimes the cost of rehabilitating 'could use' material outweighs the educational benefit that the material had in the first place. However, if the determination is there, then this material will have to be treated in the same manner as the material in the suitable pile.

To build this material into your instruction process you will need to consider the three incorporating strategies outlined below. All material that you want to use in a course must be integrated with the course presentation.

'Before' strategies

Here you, as appraiser, should provide some information on the strategies that could be used with the material. These strategies will have arisen during the 'steps' analysis.

For example, it is unlikely that the material will be without a flaw. Therefore strategies will be needed to incorporate the material into the instruction process and to optimize the impact of the material in that process. However, should you be lucky enough to find unflawed material this material will need strategies to prepare the students for the presentation and for follow-up activities.

Strategies used to introduce material include advance organizers, defining tasks and scene-setting or other activities to get learners thinking about what it is they know and what it is they are about to experience. Sometimes this is called 'promoting mathemagenic behaviour'.

'During' strategies

Strategies to be used as the material is being presented include stopping and discussing the action or the information that the learner has just seen. This has the effect of grounding the new information into what the learner already knows. Tasks such as note-taking may be set, but care needs to be taken so that the note-taking does not lead to distraction or confusion, particularly if the pace of the material is fast. Parts of the material may be skipped if they are not relevant.

'After' strategies

Strategies after using the material should include activities that add value to the material. Frequently material is shown and then not linked or made relevant to current studies; it is as if the mere process of presenting the material is enough. This is not the case and activities need to be developed that clearly indicate to the learner the significance of the material.

These resource-appraisal techniques are summarized in Figure 5.1.

What are the objectives of this lesson/course?

Title of video or material

Does this material support all or some of those objectives?

Yes

Is the presentation of content 'clear'   No   *Discard*

Yes

Is the information and practice shown up-to-date?   No   *Discard*

Yes   Is it of 'historical' interest
                 and is this important?
        No
                              Yes

Does the material present the content in a   No   *Discard*
logical manner and with reasonable timing or
pace?

                No Is there a strategy you could use
Yes   to overcome this?   No   *Discard*
                                Yes

Is the material at the right level for the students?

Yes   No
                    Would an introduction or
Does the material have   explanation solve the problem?
any other bad points?
                                          No   *Discard*

                                No   *Decide on effectiveness*
Yes
Can you reduce the effect of the
bad points?

                                No   *Discard*
Yes
What strategies can   Strategies before
be used to reduce
the bad points? →   Strategies during

                             Strategies after

The strategies to be used evolve through the use of the algorithm and are therefore included as part of the worksheet for the algorithm. The title of the material and the objectives are inputs into the algorithm.

Figure 5.1   *An algorithm to test the effectiveness of material*

CONCLUSION

Be clear about what it is you are looking for. This will be based on the information you have collected elsewhere.

List the materials as you view or review them, noting information like cost, year of production and any copyright considerations. This information will tell you if the material is too costly, out-of-date or too difficult to obtain.

As you view or review the materials, be ruthless. We recognize that there are lots of things that it would be nice to have in teaching materials. The reality is there are only so many hours in the day and there would be a lot of work involved in making 'nice' appropriate and the 'interesting' relevant.

Some items that you view or review will immediately be seen as not appropriate. Discard these and do not revisit this pile. One review panel ended up with all the material in the reject pile. They started to go back over this discarded material. When questioned why, they said they felt guilty that they didn't like anything. We were able to put the information on what they *did not like* to good use in developing specifications for what *they did like*.

Most review panels end up with a 'possible' pile and 'yes' pile. The 'yes' pile, if it exists at all, will consist of one or two items only. The 'possible' pile may have more items in it. Generally speaking the discussion will then start on how best to redevelop or adapt the materials. Before this discussion goes too far, look at the information on production, date and copyright. Let's say the material was produced four years ago. If you are planning a minimum of five years self-life for the course you are developing, this material will be almost ten years old by the end. How dated it will look then is difficult to predict. More importantly, the information it contains may need to be modified in just a few years' time. The main point to be aware of if using material from the 'possible' pile is that you could be building in obsolescence.

For people experienced in evaluation, these steps may seem unnecessary or some of us may see them as intuitive. However, for new evaluators the relationship between the material and providing some form of advice may not be clear. The steps outlined here are intended to be of use to those moving into resource evaluation. In our experience, most evaluation sheets tend to ask questions about the content or have some form of graded checklist, and then ask for some evaluation statement. The steps outlined here could be incorporated into those sheets, or used as a guide to develop evaluation statements.

The need to clarify objectives provides a base for determining the usefulness of the material under review. This, combined with the need to determine strategies through the evaluation process, sees early decisions about the suitability of the material, leading to discarding the material as unsuitable for the objectives, or choosing incorporating strategies if the material has redeeming merit. As such the process not only determines suitability but also provides possible actions to incorporate the material appropriately into a course.

The real problem with evaluating resources for appropriateness is that few if any of the evaluations are disseminated within or across organizations. The value of this process is in assisting people to make decisions about materials and to determine strategies for their appropriate use in teaching. Hopefully the evaluations you make will not languish on a shelf like so many useful resources because those they would benefit are not informed of their existence.

Chapter 6
Some Management Tips for a New Course or New Material

SUMMARY

Developing new materials for a new course frequently requires teachers to work with people who are not teachers or trainers. These people are experts in print production, audio-visual materials and other media such as computers. At issue here is how educators and trainers communicate with production personnel who in most cases are not expert in the content of the materials being developed.

INTRODUCTION

It is assumed that the documentation for the course, including a list of the resources needed for delivery, is complete. If the resources you need do not exist there is a need to translate the documentation into a form that the producers of the material will understand, which will require you to specify the content of the resources for the course.

This may mean you working with production people who are not educators. Their views on production needs may be based on commercial production values. These need not be in conflict with educational needs, but there is a danger that 'glitz', as the production value, could override the educational and training message.

This leads to the following questions that you will need to answer:

- How do you develop criteria for the development of new teaching and/or learner materials by resource production personnel? (These people may be independent of your organization).
- What are the steps you need to take to make sure that the materials produced will be applicable to the teaching and learning in the course? This raises quality assurance issues.
- What are the pitfalls of working with non-educators and trainers to develop the resource materials and how can you avoid them?

It is assumed that the resources to be developed go beyond the day-to-day resources that most teachers prepare to support or supplement materials that might be provided. The materials discussed here could be course notes for learners, video, or computer-based materials.

We have come across situations where, when a teacher has requested a resource production department to develop new resources, he or she has been asked, 'What already exists, why doesn't it meet your need and what is unique in your proposal?' – and the teacher has felt confronted. This should not be the case. In asking these questions, the production people are trying to establish if they are being asked to 'reinvent the wheel', in producing another version of material that already exists and could fit the requirement.

In reality such questions help to determine the real need for new resources; they also allow the production people to determine the demands on their time that the production of this material could make, in the light of their current workloads. For you, this is an important factor because if your project overloads the production people, your materials may not see 'the light of day' when you expect them. There will also be consideration of the best use of resources in developing a large-scale production or a smaller-scale production to meet a 'local' need.

In many organizations there are resource development departments or units. In some of these, the people will have an educational background, sometimes they will not and it is more than likely that some will have industrial/commercial experience. Using people with a commercial background in developing education and training material is often justified on the grounds of production efficiency.

Requests for new material come from real need – or do they?

In many cases the chance to develop a new course entices people to become involved in the development of new course materials.

However, a commitment to plan, develop and participate in the production of new resource materials for a course should only be made after an appraisal of available resources has established that existing materials will not do, for whatever reason.

The appraisal of available resources to support the delivery of the course means that you have looked around, and sought advice from librarians and suppliers of educational and training programmes (this is covered in Chapter 4). You have reviewed material from catalogues and perhaps from similar schools, colleges or institutions, but nothing fits your needs for teaching or for the learners. It is only when no available resource materials seem appropriate for use in the course that you are planning that you are faced with the need to have material produced.

You may find some appropriate resources for part of the course and you might be able to negotiate to 'buy' this material. This means that there is only a need to produce the teaching and learning materials to fill the 'gaps' in the resources.

If you have searched for material that might make the course more comprehensible, be it a video, a still photo or a computer simulation, and the conclusion is that there is none, you are faced with the task of approaching someone to produce this material for you. What do you do? The first thing is don't panic!

TWO BACKGROUND ORGANIZATIONAL CONSIDERATIONS

If you are faced with the production of new course support materials then there is a strong likelihood that you are going to have to talk to production people. If you have all the skills and abilities and in-house production facilities then perhaps you don't need to read this chapter. However, if these facilities are not available 'in-house', you will need to read this chapter. In this chapter it is not possible to cover all the permutations of what must be remembered if you are using people outside your organization. What you must remember is that you are in a real client/service relationship. You have a need; these people must provide you with a service to satisfy it.

Remember you are involved as the project developer and you, along with any team, have determined the need. You have documentation, such as a Course Information Document (CID). If you have reviewed existing resources, you have reports that indicate you've looked for, but not found, appropriate material to fill your needs. This documentation, the review of available material and some of the steps in this chapter will have prepared you to meet these production people.

SOME BACKGROUND ON COMMERCIAL PRODUCTION COMPANIES AND IN-HOUSE PRODUCTION UNITS

The comparative ability of commercial production companies and in-house production units to come up with material you require is something you will have to judge.

Your role with commercial producers and/or in-house producers is to make sure that the material you want developed is fit for your purpose. This, after all, is what the production of quality material is all about. However, while the relationship with commercial producers and in-house producers is that of client/supplier, the relationship between you and an outside production house may be different to the relationship you have with in-house production people. The relationship with a commercial supplier is based on contracts and real money changing hands. In the in-house setting, however, you may be competing with others for the scare resources available to the whole institution. As such, the brief you prepare for the production of the materials in-house will probably need to cover a few extra issues if in-house production is to be used.

The extra questions your brief needs to cover for in-house production relate to a general set of criteria:

- On what grounds, basis or rationale is this teaching or learning resource material required?
- Is there anything like this material on the market/available elsewhere? This question makes sense if the materials are required 'in-house'.
- What are the comparative costs of having the material produced outside the organization (commonly called 'outsourcing')?
- What is your budget?
- What is your deadline?

Using the information you have gathered you will be able to answer the questions as follows.

Use your course information document and the learner profile as your main source of information here.

On what grounds, basis or rationale is this material required?

If you have followed some of the advice about collecting course information in a CID, as set out in other parts of this book and a companion volume, *Planning a Course*, you probably have an excellent idea of what you want and do not want. You will be able to provide examples of the format of presentation of material, even if the content of the example is not appropriate. This information helps production people focus on your intentions.

Is there anything like this on the market/available elsewhere?

If you have reviewed existing material you will be able to say why it does not fit your criteria. Having the answers to these two questions will help you in your next task which is to describe what it is you want. If you can describe it then perhaps it can be made.

It will cost; what is your budget?

The course specification documents and the associated documents will give you an indication of budget for the overall project. What the production people want to know is if there is a budget to produce these materials.

What is your deadline?

These production people are really asking a question to help them. If your time line is short this could skew some of their other work and upset other clients they are working for. If your time line is not too tight, then your project could be 'fitted in' around the existing workload.

Some points to remember

Table 6.1 indicates the time and activities involved in producing various materials. You should note that this is for an hour of finished material. If you are producing considerably more than this, some of the time spent on consulting and development of specifications will be attributed to all the material. The chart is a guide and it is in hours. You will have to determine the cost in your currency. What the chart does

Table 6.1   *Time and activities involved in producing materials*

Type of technology	Product	Description of content of product	Main activities	Hours to finished product-ratio
Print	Workbook	Examples	Planning Writing or typing and printing	1:10
	Distance education course	Teaching notes and workbook	Desktop publishing Subject expert or tutor	1:20
Video	Stand alone	Video	Scriptwriter Production crew and editing	1:40
	Kit	Video and support notes	Scriptwriter Production crew Support materials	1:50
Computer	CML	Test item bank	Developing test bank items and validating them	1:80
	CBT	Teaching materials plus test items	Developing the script Authoring Developing the test bank and validating	1:150 (this may be too low)
CD Rom	Interactive	Integrated materials	Developing the script Authoring and building the resource data-base Developing the test bank and validating	1:200

indicate is that the more 'high tech' the product, the greater the cost, in time and money. For example it is possible to produce print materials in the time indicated in the table. However, this time will increase and the costs explode if the materials are to be produced with colour printing or photographs.

The table may also help you determine some of the information required for the technical (rather than the educational) specifications for the material you require.

Unless you are up to date on the latest media, avoid specifying a particular medium or technology.

All educational decisions must be based on the course documents. This will ensure that the outcome of the production process fits your needs. There are many decisions that need to be made, but while you are defining what you need, avoid the temptation to predetermine the media you will use. Remember that not all media are appropriate for all education and training tasks and some media are more appropriate to some education and training tasks than others. Elsewhere we talk about some of the limitations that the use of certain media might impose in terms of access and equity issues. Therefore avoid media decisions in initially describing what you want from the materials. Let your description of 'information need' define the media that might be used.

STAGES IN DEVELOPING YOUR DESCRIPTION OF THE MATERIALS YOU NEED

Where to start

Make sure that your production plan is a viable one by checking it out with the production people.

The first thing to do is determine the time line you have for production. If you have a tight schedule, then you don't have much time for anything other than a rudimentary production of resources. The longer the lead time the better. If you need it tomorrow then... (you probably know the answer).

When you start this list of information remember that you are the expert in your *content*. The people you are working with have expertise in *production*. If you feel that these print, video or computing experts are ignoring your needs, then try and find examples that could be used to indicate your expectations.

Faced with a blank sheet of paper, the first thing to do is to write down what the outcome of using this material will be. Just as courses have outcomes, so too does the use of materials in the course. If in doubt refer back to the course specification form and related documents.

As the content expert, start by listing the expected outcome(s) of the materials you are producing.

With the 20:20 vision of hindsight it is easy to write, 'the first thing to do is to list the expected outcomes'. But if it is the first time you have done it, then budget for several sheets of paper before you are 'happy'.

When you are 'happy', try to draft out some details. Here 'draft' means a few words or a brief description of content concepts in an order that they might be. The danger is that these descriptions become too detailed and you end up with a very long briefing document. Yes, 'briefing document', because that is what you are developing. A briefing document contains all the information that the people, including yourself, need to be clear about before production of the materials starts. If this seems like a lot of bother, remember that without an agreed core document, mistakes, delays and frustrations will occur that take years off people's allotted span of humour, tolerance and flexibility.

Remember that not all production people are educators or trainers so you must make clear your outcomes. If you don't, the outcome could be their version of what you require.

As the content expert, take a moment to outline what the content should look like to achieve the outcome(s).

What you should include in the description and why

Descriptions can include:

- *Content references* – these are important for setting the parameters of the course for all the people involved. It may be important to include references to what is not needed.
- *Visual references* – these can include content, desired detail and what you want to show.
- *Flow of information* – this could include the relationship of one point of information to the next or related information.
- *Sources or sites of information* – these could include known or suspected sources of material that reduce the cost of production. The use of this material may involve copyright considerations.

Remember to remain realistic

How important is the content of this material to the course? If the material you want to develop is a minimal part of the course, then you should devote a relatively small portion of time to it so that you can concentrate your time and efforts on the development of the major part of the materials.

How much time will it take to develop the materials? What is your lead time, or the time you have between now and when you require the materials? There are some 'nice' things to consider such as trialling the material so that you are confident that it does what you want it to do. Lead time will also be affected by the time it takes to produce material that might be incorporated into the final set of materials. As an example, a short video took 36 hours to produce; the support booklet took twice as long, because some shots from the video were needed for the booklet. In effect, the production of the booklet had to stop until the video was shot.

Typically, learning materials have a shelf life of only two or three years so make sure that you plan accordingly.

In consultation on the preparation of the material you must consider the volatility of the material. What is its shelf-life? Teaching material is often a perishable material: changes in knowledge and/or techniques can make it redundant.

If we look at distance education materials that have to be kept reasonably up-to-date, the shelf-life of most materials in most institutions that we know about is five years. That is, the course material that they are sending out to students is reviewed for possible updating on a five-year rotation. Depending on the subject, some material will only require minor changes, even after five years, and in most cases this updating is to provide more recent examples. In other subjects such as computing, some course content is so volatile that an almost constant upgrading of material is required.

In the face-to-face teaching setting, many teachers review their material on an annual basis, because most courses in primary and secondary-middle schools are year-long efforts. In training, courses may have several offerings in a calendar year and therefore may be subject to more frequent review. There is the story, possibly apocryphal, for the teacher boasting in the staff room that they had been teaching for 20 years. When the teacher left, another teacher said in a stage whisper, 'Actually, that person has been teaching only one year, but the same year 20 times'.

THE PITFALLS

There are pitfalls for the developer of new materials when 'external' production people are involved. The first of these is the seduction from your intent.

An example which could apply equally to large departments in colleges and universities sets the scene. A group of teachers in several schools decided, following a moderation process, that they wanted some print and photographic materials that they could share as a common resource. Consultation took place with a person to produce these, and raw material was provided by the teachers for the development of the materials. What was delivered was a video tape using the visual material and a voice-over based very loosely on the text material. It was usable, so long as the students had a video replay machine. It was not as specified and the clients never used that 'service' facility again.

How do you overcome such a pitfall? The simple answer is to establish a client/service relationship as soon as possible. In many institutions this may not be necessary – but you may not know this is the case if you are new to an institution. So be warned. But also be warned that in many schools, colleges and institutions, some of the support people have been there for many years. Some of these people have their best attempts to support new ideas, curriculum change and the best laid plans of mice and people go down the drain. Why? Because the people who suggested the scheme were promoted or moved on and there was no infrastructure for ongoing support – and ongoing support for the programme or innovation is essential. Therefore you need to develop and put in place an infrastructure of support, just in case anything happens to you, such as promotion, invitation to a new job, etc. But that infrastructure really has nothing to do with you – it is about supporting learners to ensure that if anything does happen to you, they will not be left high and dry.

The second pitfall is 'blowing out' of the materials from your intent. If you are a first-time developer this could be a particularly nasty pitfall. It's nasty because your idea of the need for this material and the development process will be taken over by non-educator production people who will impose their edict that the materials will be delivered by..., and generally add glamour without adding quality. You can kiss goodbye to the simple solution to your immediate problem.

You as a 'new player' could be seen by the production people as not 'understanding' the production process. This may be true: you might not understand the production process – but you do *know* the materials you want. In this situation you might point out that you are the client and if these production people cannot deliver to your specifications then there are other options. This is confrontational, but it may be necessary to achieve the product you want.

As a new player the one safeguard you have is your documentation. The documentation indicates what is needed, and can be used to support your argument for what you need against someone else's idea of what they want to produce. This documentation could include the size of the client group, costs, the number of times used – in fact the information you would have on a CID.

As a new player you could develop a reference group or working party, or a discussion group may be able to work out a more realistic solution to encroaching on your project.

There are other problems that arise at the time of development. The first of these is a change in curriculum. This is highly unlikely if the course specification form has been thorough. However, it can happen anywhere that there is volatile content. Such changes need not be disastrous but they can cause the odd sleepless night as you work to make the necessary modifications. The real problem is that these changes are seldom documented and this can lead to mistakes and misunderstandings about what is being changed and why. If the changes are major, then the simple advice is cut your losses – but don't run. Document why the project had to be abandoned.

The second problem is associated with people. This can range from simple over-commitment of people who find themselves short of time, to the other extreme of lack of commitment and people not putting in the effort required. Sometimes people move on and this can disrupt the process until a new member is found and 'brought up to speed'. Often there is no new member found and the busy people become even busier.

There are also problems associated with resources. Promised resources are not made available. This seldom happens, but backers have been known to withdraw support. A more common problem arises with a project that spans two financial years and the assumption, or promise, is made that completion funding will be available from the following financial year. What happens when the assumption, or promise, does not eventuate?

CONCLUSION

In preparing new materials, documentation by you (and/or your team) is one of the best safeguards to ensure the development of courses and course support materials that are appropriate for the needs you have identified.

The relationship between course developers and educational and training materials providers needs to be focused on the education and training, not the production values.

Chapter 7
Innovation: Preparing the Materials

SUMMARY

This chapter considers preparing the material for an innovation, but in doing so we also look at the organizational culture and how it can be a barrier to change. The reasons why people resist change and three ways of changing people's attitudes – education, participation and support – are discussed. The chapter also looks at the advantages of having an implementation plan for a programme. Finally, the chapter describes the ways in which learners can be prepared for change.

INTRODUCTION

When considering preparing materials for an innovation, we must look at the total innovation, not just the material alone. Even if we have excellent materials, the innovation can still fail if it is not implemented correctly.

Try to make both your education and training more flexible and responsive to the learner by making the materials learner focused.

The use of mass instruction and, to a lesser extent, group instruction, can hardly be called innovative as they are already widely used. However, individualized instruction or flexible and open learning are now beginning to enjoy wider acceptance because of the changing needs of learners, education and training. There is a recognition that in education and training there is a need to be more process-based and flexible in delivery instruction. Knowledge is increasing at such a rapid rate that workers must continually update their knowledge or risk becoming redundant. Innovations, such as open learning, allow learning materials to be delivered in a flexible manner when and where they are needed.

In this chapter the implementation of a small-scale innovation will be described. Perhaps you will be individualizing one of your modules; if you are, then the procedure outlined in this chapter should assist you.

Course materials are an essential component of an innovative programme, such as open learning, but often there is no implementation plan for them. The course materials must be considered in the wider implementation plan of the programme, otherwise the programme will be doomed to failure.

ORGANIZATIONAL CULTURE

Every organization has its own unique culture, and it is important that you are aware of it and understand it if you are to implement change. To understand what your organizational culture is, ask yourself the following questions:

Every organization has its own unique culture. Consider conducting an organizational profile to generate information regarding the current culture in your organization.

- What is the nature of your work?
- How many distinct groups of people (cultures) are there in your organization?
- What is your organization's mission statement and corporate goals?
- What type of organizational structure operates?
- What is your organization's style of management?
- What are the characteristics of the staff in your organization?
- What shared values do all the staff have in your organization?
- What are the decision-making characteristics of your organization?
- What is the technology orientation of your organization?
- Does your organization take risks?
- What is the remuneration philosophy of your organization?
- How is work planned and monitored in your organization?
- Is there staff development in your organization?
- What is promotion based on in your organization?
- How are objectives or targets set in your organization?
- How 'open' is communication in your organization?

Your answers to these questions will provide you with a good idea of your organization's culture. Different types of culture may be influenced and changed by different types of strategies used to implement change. An understanding of your organization's culture should assist you in implementing your innovation by helping you identify who is likely to resist your innovation and the appropriate strategies for overcoming this opposition.

CULTURAL CHANGE

Changing the organizational culture of a traditional educational institute from a lecture/tutorial model to a more flexible delivery method requires a radical shift in the culture and that will not be easily done without a detailed implementation strategy or plan. Before you can develop your implementation plan you must identify who will resist change, and how this opposition can be overcome.

Flexible delivery methods of instruction often require a radical shift in organizational culture. Make sure that you are well prepared.

Why do people resist change?

People resist change for three basic reasons:

- people are afraid of change, they are more comfortable with the status quo
- people fear that they do not have the skills and/or knowledge to cope with the change
- people can see how the change will affect them and they don't like what they see.

Who might resist change?

When implementing any change in an organization, many people are affected. Virtually anybody can resist the implementation of change. For example:

If teachers do not support the innovation then it will never be successful no matter how good it is. Make sure that you have good support for whatever it is that you are doing.

- teachers can resist change because they have prepared materials to be delivered in a particular manner and any change would mean additional work for them
- laboratory technicians can resist change simply because it would require extra work in the laboratory or workshop
- administrators may believe the introduction of some innovation may make administration more complex or costly

- learners may feel that they are doing some of their teacher's work
- potential employers may feel that learners will not reach the required level of competence
- the wider community may see the change as an erosion of educational standards
- traditional institutions may believe it is just another change for change's sake by trendy institutions.

Whatever the reason people have for opposing change, you must try to alter their attitudes and relieve their fears; if you don't, there is a danger of your innovation failing.

OVERCOMING THE OPPOSITION

To identify the potential problems of implementing an innovation you should determine why an innovation is required and why it is not seen as necessary by some. For example, an innovation may be necessary because:

- the administration wants it implemented
- there is a need to improve the quality of learning
- there are training problems that are not being met successfully by traditional education
- courses have falling enrolments
- there is pressure to increase your organization's enrolment with little or no corresponding increase in physical or financial resources
- the teaching staff would like to change
- there is a need for the courses to be delivered in a more flexible manner
- industry requires the change to improve its potential workers' skills.

The innovation may not be seen as necessary by some because:

- there is a lack of relevant expertise in the skills required for the innovation
- there are no additional funds available
- learners may be resistant to different teaching/learning methods
- your physical resources may not be suitable for anything but the lecture/tutorial method.

You may be fortunate in having many reasons for implementing an innovation and few reasons for not. However, usually the two are more equally balanced. To implement an innovation you must increase the reasons for the change and weaken the reasons against it; the strategies to do this will be discussed later.

CHANGING ATTITUDES

When innovating any teaching/learning method there will be some people in favour, some neutral and some against the change. If you are implementing an innovation it is your role to change the attitudes of those who are neutral and against the change, but remember, it will be unlikely that you will change everyone's attitude. There are three methods of changing people's attitude:

- education
- participation
- support

Education

There are two ways to educate staff and learners about change: selling the benefits of the innovation, and staff development.

Selling the benefits

Selling the benefits of your innovation should start well before it is implemented. Conducting information sessions for the staff, and at a later stage for the learners, about the benefits of the innovation will allow people to discuss their fears and apprehensions about the programme.

Here are some examples of how you can approach these sessions:

- explain why the programme is required and who wants the change
- state the advantages and disadvantages of the innovation
- present an implementation plan, preferably a written document, but one that is flexible enough that it can be changed at a later stage
- outline cases where the programme has been successfully implemented in similar circumstances
- present the findings of relevant research
- allow for discussion and questions about the innovation.

Other methods of selling the benefits of the innovation include:

● arranging for visits by staff to places where the innovation is already in operation
● having teachers working in a similar programme speak to the staff at meetings or seminars
● writing papers for the relevant journals and newsletters on the innovation
● talking informally, whenever you get the opportunity, about the innovation.

When selling the benefits of the innovation you must never make any false claims about it as this will ultimately be a hindrance to you.

Staff development

Staff development can be very effective in changing people's attitude to an innovation, but it must involve more than just selling the benefits. Staff development must be directed at giving the participants particular skills and knowledge they will need to implement the innovation. There are many approaches to staff development and the type you choose will depend on the type of innovation you are trying to implement.

Staff development for the implementation of innovation can be designed so that participants use the innovation method for the staff development activity itself. Integrating the participants' work environment into the staff development activity makes it more effective because the participants can see that it is directly relevant. You may have group discussions on a topic and ask participants to complete a relevant activity using the innovative materials you have provided them with. This has the added advantage of allowing the participants to see what it is like to study the new method.

You should allow for discussion and questions, as the staff development activity is about changing the staff's attitudes as much as giving them specific competences. The traditional staff development activity of withdrawing staff for one or two days can be very effective, but there are other types of staff development activities which can also be useful. These include:

● having staff undertake a formal professional qualification in the innovative method
● having the staff involved in a pilot project on the innovation

- releasing staff for periods of employment in another institution using the innovation you are considering
- releasing staff for professional development related to the innovation.

Staff development can be critical in the effective implementation of your innovation and you should use a variety of staff development programmes to assist you.

Participation

Your programme will be more effectively implemented if the staff participate at all levels of management and decision making. Participation means that staff are involved through:

- sharing ownership
- taking part in the decision making
- being kept informed.

Sharing ownership

Sharing ownership involves the staff considering the programme as their own. To share ownership, the staff must believe there are advantages in implementing the programme for them, the learners and the administration. To ensure shared ownership you may have to modify your innovation. If the staff indicate they will not accept your initial innovation proposal, you will have to re-examine your position. In this way they will share ownership of the modified proposal.

Successful innovations are usually championed by an individual or group participating in the project. Make sure that you use these people to the best advantage.

Taking part in decision making

An open style of management is most effective in implementing an innovation. This will involve the staff participating in the decision making and a collegial type of management (shared responsibility). Not all decisions need to be made by the team; there will be decisions that need to be made quickly and they are not worth calling a meeting for. But the major decisions should be made by the group, on a consensus basis.

Communicate with the staff

To keep the staff informed you must communicate with them regularly. If the staff are 'kept in the dark' about implementing the programme, this will breed distrust and anxiety. Methods to inform the staff include:

● regular progress meetings
● newsletters on the progress of the programme
● documentation on who is doing what
● informal communications with the staff on the latest development.

If staff are kept well informed then they will fear the innovation less and feel they are an essential part of the programme, which they are. Communication with staff should be a high priority for the effective implementation of any innovation.

Support

If teachers are given little support for implementing an innovation, there is a chance it will fail. How an innovation can be supported will vary depending on the type of innovation it is.

The administration and management of an educational institute can support teachers in implementing an innovation by providing:

● funds for course development
● time release for staff to develop and implement the innovation
● support staff to assist in developing training materials
● an understanding management
● flexible administration
● learning facility for learners
● the equipment required for learning and development
● library facilities suitable for the innovation.

Support is essential for the implementation of an innovative programme. If you have succeeded in changing any negative staff attitudes toward your programme, these people will quickly become disillusioned if they think they are doing all the work with very little support.

CASE STUDY

Effective innovations sometimes fail because people have not developed an implementation strategy or plan. An implementation strategy is different from the development of course materials.

A good place to start developing an implementation strategy is to consider the characteristics of the innovation you are trying to implement and determine where you are now, where you want to be and how you are going to get there.

Rather than consider a case in abstract we will consider a more practical example and see how you can develop an implementation plan.

In this example, you want to implement a more open type of learning in a large, traditional tertiary institute which has many courses and students. There are no existing learning materials apart from lecture notes, and most of the staff use the traditional lecture method and appear resistant to any change. The administration is conservative, but will support change provided it does not alter their administrative procedures too much.

Because of the nature of the change, you realize that implementing open learning will take many years. Table 7.1 provides you with a start to developing your implementation plan. It shows the elements of the open learning programme you want to implement, where you are now and where you want to be.

From the information in the table you can now develop the goals you must achieve to implement open learning in your institute. Once you have done this, your next task is to develop some strategies that will enable you to achieve these objectives. Since the organization is large

Make sure that you conduct a field trial before you try to implement any major innovation.

Table 7.1 *Implementation plan*

Element of open learning	Where we are now	Where we want to be
Orientation	Teacher-centred	Learner-centred
Course pattern	Fixed	Negotiable with the teacher
Method of instruction	Teachers	Learner has some choice
Pacing	Lock step (fixed)	Self-pacing
Main learning	From lecturers, tutorial and lecture notes	From a variety of learning materials
Subject length	Year level	Semester (modular)
Role of teachers	Information-givers	Facilitators of learning
Communication	One-way	Two-way
Enrolment	Fixed	Flexible (variable)

and to move it from a traditional lecture/tutorial method to open learning requires a major change, you may decide to develop a two-year plan and accept the partial implementation of open learning. The type of *objectives* you may develop to implement open learning over a two-year period are as follows:

- establish how the institute will use open learning to make teaching and learning more efficient
- identify areas where the institute could use open learning to give it a competitive edge in the education market
- establish an open learning philosophy which is suitable for the institute
- create a climate of interest in open learning in the staff, students and other clients
- have the majority of the staff in favour of open learning
- establish a format and style of open learning module which is suitable for implementation at the institute
- have a method of managing open learning firmly in place
- have at least one subject operating in the open learning mode.

Now the objectives have been determined you need to plan how you are going to achieve these objectives. Here are some suggested strategies:

- providing information on open learning
- putting in place a computer-managed learning system
- developing an open learning module format
- developing one module in the open learning mode
- finding areas where open learning can be used
- sourcing existing open learning materials for use in the institute.

Information on open learning

Conduct regular half-day workshops for the staff on open learning. The topics covered in the workshops could include:

- What is open learning?
- The advantages of open learning.
- The disadvantages of open learning.
- Why use open learning?
- Where open learning is being used.
- How to implement open learning.
- How to manage open learning.

These workshops will provide staff with background information about open learning. The course could be adapted for presentations to students and other interested groups.

Computer-managed learning

In open learning the management of student learning is difficult because students are all working at their own rate, so some type of computer assistance can be extremely effective in managing the programme. Computer-managed learning (CML) is a system used to track students through a series of predefined learning activities.

Conduct CML courses for staff and students to show them the advantages and disadvantages of CML and how it can be used with open learning.

Open learning module format

Determine what format of open learning modules would be most suitable for the institute.

Develop one module in the open learning mode

One module suitable for open learning and where the staff are keen to develop open learning materials should be identified. This module would then operate in the open learning mode and be supported by a range of multimedia and managed by CML. This model could then be used as an example of what can be done with open learning and provide a 'selling point' for staff, students and other clients.

Once the module has been identified, an open learning development team must be established. The team may consist of the following members:

- two subject matter experts from the relevant departments
- two instructional designers
- one computer-based training representative
- one media representative
- one teaching methods adviser
- one graphic artist
- one evaluator.

This team would be responsible for implementing the programme.

Find areas where open learning can be used

Determine areas where open learning can be used most effectively. Some areas of industry training should be suitable, where the students are no longer required to be on campus to complete theory, practical work or examinations. This would appeal to employers and students in terms of saving time and money and in added convenience. Ideally, learners would be using open learning materials and completing testing requirements and communications via CML. These areas would be determined by a management team.

Source existing open learning materials

There is a wide range of open learning materials available and some of these may be suitable for the institute. If any existing learning materials are applicable, this would save a great deal of time and money.

Time lines

Now the objective and strategies have been developed, you should turn your attention to time lines. These time lines should be set by the open learning management team which would monitor each of the strategies. Definite dates should be given as to when the strategies would be implemented.

1. Information on open learning
   - conduct at least four courses per year starting in January
2. Computer-managed learning
   - complete investigations and make recommendations by June
   - conduct at least three CML courses per year
3. Open learning module format
   - determine the format by December
4. Establish an open learning module
   - start development in June and have it operational in June the following year
5. Find areas where open learning can be used
   - complete the initial recommendations by September; continuous process
6. Source existing open learning materials
   - complete the initial investigation by October; continuous process.

This two-year implementation plan will assist you in introducing the programme, but the plan should be constantly reviewed and updated as required. At the end of two years another plan should be developed for a longer time frame. This is called a stabilization plan, where you outline strategies for the on-going support of the programme.

Although the innovation considered here is open learning, a similar strategy can be used for any innovation. When developing your own implementation plan:

- decide where you are now and where you want to be
- develop some objectives you want to achieve in the time frame you are considering
- develop strategies to achieve these objectives
- develop time lines.

THE LEARNER

We have discussed how to implement your innovation and how the attitude of teaching staff may be changed. However, there has been little reference so far to the learners. It is obviously very important that learners are considered for the effective implementation of an innovation.

How do we implement an innovative programme with the learners? Here are a few suggestions:

- inform the learners about the innovation and why it is being implemented
- explain why the innovation should benefit the learners
- conduct pilot programmes with them
- allow for special assistance when first implementing the innovation
- allow for additional learner support when the innovation is implemented on a wider scale
- conduct training programmes for the learner on the additional skills they will require for the innovation
- be prepared to adapt the innovation to suit the learner.

Since the innovation is usually for the benefit of learners they must be considered when implementing the innovation.

CONCLUSION

The implementation of any innovation is never easy, especially with something as complex as open learning. The development of an implementation plan will assist you greatly with the smooth implementation of an innovation. The implementation phase of a project can be critical and be the 'make or break' point of the project; this is why care must be taken.

Chapter 8

Preparing On-line Learning Materials

SUMMARY

The use of computers and communication technologies in learning has a history going back at least 30 years. In that time it has been called by many names, including computer mediated communication (CMC), computer conferencing, telematics, on-line learning, and more recently, internet based learning. With the advent of the World Wide Web and organization based intranets a new and interesting environment for technology based learning has been created that offers many new possibilities without some of the problems that have been present in older computer-based learning applications.

This chapter is an overview of some of the many issues you should consider when developing on-line learning materials.

INTRODUCTION

An on-line learning or virtual classroom is something that can be created within a World Wide Web environment and accessed via a local area network (LAN) that has been developed within your organization or college campus. An on-line classroom is a mechanism for distributing information to your learners and performing other tasks related to communication, assessment and classroom management.

Many of the tools that provide the functionality of the on-line classroom use a variety of computer applications along with a simple interface that allows your learners to access and use the required learning materials.

On-line learning classrooms can be used for anything that your existing networks are used for, however, through the use of particular kinds of software learners are able to collaborate on projects and share information. A variety of specialized software technologies is also available that allows for the customization of applications to the needs of an organization.

DEVELOPING LEARNING MATERIALS

The development of on-line learning materials is, for the most part, no different from the development of print based or other technology based learning materials discussed throughout this book, in that they should all use a four phase systematic development strategy.

When developing materials for on-line learning, however, your production phase will now include an authoring phase along with the loading and testing of your learning materials into the on-line system.

THE ON-LINE CLASSROOM

In an on-line classroom environment the materials development phase will involve the setting up of computers for learner use, preparing new learning materials and converting existing materials, creating quizzes, setting up class and mailing lists, drawing or scanning pictures, digitizing video and developing audio files. In some cases you might also be involved in the setting up of a computer managed learning system to assist in tracking your learners through various learning events and the marking of quizzes and examinations.

When considering a computer managed learning (CML) system, ensure that it is web enabled and compatible with the other applications you are using.

After your learning materials have been developed and produced they are typically stored on one or more computers or servers. The stored information can be in a variety of forms such as HTML and other application based pages, sound files, graphics or video. These computers 'serve' as the distribution points for your learning materials. Anyone wanting to access these materials can do so from their own desktop or laptop computer.

Having learning materials stored in a server means that they can be searched, archived, indexed and converted easily and quickly. On many servers there are also a variety of applications that your learners need in order to complete the learning prescribed for them.

Client programs, or programs that are used by both yourself as a teacher or facilitator and, your learners, are programs that ask other programs, such as those running in a wide area network (WAN) environment, to perform various tasks such as getting information or sending messages. These programs also provide the learners with the means of accessing the information that you have stored on local servers as well as accessing other network servers.

CLIENT, SERVER AND SUPPORT SOFTWARE

A large collection of software has been developed to help you design, develop and maintain the daily activity of an on-line classroom. One way of grouping this software is to use the following three categories:

- **Support** – software in this category generally has little or no direct connection outside of your local area network. This is software your learners use to support their activity within the on-line classroom. Some examples include word processors, graphics programs, and databases.
- **Client** – your learners participate in the on-line classroom environment via a computer and a collection of client software. This client software provides the interface between them and the on-line classroom. Examples of client software could include e-mail applications and programs such as Top Class where your learners can come together and engage in various learning activities. In some virtual classroom environments such as Persyst, for example, you can give 'live lectures' in the 'classroom', your learners can complete their assignments at 'their desk' and group assignments can be completed in 'breakout rooms'. In this kind of virtual learning environment your learners can work together (synchronous mode) or individually (asynchronous mode) at any time of the day.
- **Server** – client software provides the interface that allows the learner to see and use the learning materials, but it does not provide a method for managing and distributing the information required to allow a group of learners to communicate and share information. Management and distribution of information in an on-line based classroom is the responsibility of server software.

Like your choice of CML system, make sure that your choice of virtual classroom software is compatible with the other applications you are using. Spend a lot of time researching your needs.

Typically the computer the on-line learner has on his or her desk provides both the support and client software, while the server software resides on one or two central computers. However, it is quite common for the developer of on-line learning materials to use one dedicated server, not accessible by the learner, as a means of storage during the development process and when completed, move the finished materials to a second server accessible by the learner. During the development stage your computer can contain all of the necessary support needed to do the development work including both client, and server software.

CONNECTIONS

For an on-line classroom to work you must have a connection between the client and server software. Some variation in the types of connection is possible. The following list breaks the possible connections into three broad categories.

- **Local area network or LAN** – many businesses and educational organizations have some form of local area network.
- **Home connections** – for most learners today, connecting from home means using a modem and a phone line. Although fast enough for most purposes, a typical (28.8 or 33.6) modem can be quite slow for the retrieval of large documents or multimedia files. This problem has been partially overcome in some parts of the world through the introduction of the 56.6 modem, ISDN lines and ASDL modems.
- **Hybrid** – in a hybrid on-line classroom you might use CD-ROM technology to distribute large amounts of basic information in a mass instructional mode along with an interface to a Web environment to provide information updates and communicate with your learners.

While the range of possibilities is almost endless, the basic rule of thumb here is 'keep it as simple as possible'.

What can be done in an on-line classroom is limited only by your imagination as the designer and your available resources. For the most part the range of possibilities is almost endless. However, as advanced as technology has become, more work is needed to ensure the learning environment is fully conducive to the needs of the learner.

Most types of learning materials can be put, in whole or in part, into an on-line learning system. The ideal materials for use in an on-line classroom are objective in nature and emphasize in-depth coverage and discussion as these can be easily supported.

The on-line classroom is suited to a learner centred role, meaning that learning information is made available for your learners to go through at their own pace and you provide the facilities that allow communication, thus encouraging them to take control of their own learning.

One of the most important things for you to understand about on-line learning is that, unlike a face-to-face learning environment, it cannot 'teach' on its own. The on-line classroom is not intended to replace you in the classroom, but merely to act as another form of learning delivery tool.

Text and graphics based on-line learning programs

Text and graphics for on-line learning should be designed whereby your learners do not simply read off the computer screen and are engaged only by the forward arrow. Any text and graphics based type of program, although not recommended for most learning should, when you require it for a very specific learning need, contain hyperlinks to other materials for further study, or to charts and graphs that further illustrate learning points. Typically, when you design screens of this nature they may contain a lower level of interactivity, but not necessarily a lower level of information.

Interactive on-line learning programs

To engage your learners with stimulating activity is both the promise and future of on-line learning. Interactivity at its best should be a simulation of the work situation and at a minimum you should include application exercises, drag and drop, column matching, testing and text entry. This type of program helps bring your learners into the materials, engage them in the content and allow them to practise the skills.

Interactive multimedia on-line learning programs

Many interactive multimedia programs allow the learner to manipulate graphic objects in real-time. The simulations are often very realistic and the situations can be difficult. Typically, interactive multimedia programs are authored using a software tool that allows for the addition of multimedia and manages high levels of interactively and record keeping. An interactive multimedia program can allow your learners to enter into a world that attempts to mimic a part of real life, providing immediate, real life responses to user input.

DESIGN AND DEVELOPMENT OF AN ON-LINE LEARNING SYSTEM

On-line learning provides a way of delivering materials to your learners that is often less expensive and more convenient than the typical alternatives. However, because this type of learning is very new, distinctions between various types of on-line learning are still forming.

When you are developing on-line learning materials and a 'system' in which to put those materials, one of the most important factors for you to consider is holding the attention of your learners and engaging their minds long enough for learning to occur. Interactivity makes the difference between the system that simply presents information and one that helps learning take place.

One of the first considerations in the design of your on-line learning system is the link between your planned network and any existing network. You will also need to review the specific learning needs of your learners and, along with the development of a graphic user interface (GUI), you will have to consider hyperlinks to the learning materials you are going to put on your system.

Also as part of this initial phase you will need to review your required learning materials and assess their viability based on delivery, treatment and various human–computer interface (HCI) issues such as media elements and the use of such materials in a technology based environment.

LEARNING MATERIALS

The use of a different medium for learning often has a significant influence on the learning that takes place and your chosen design for the on-line environment must be appropriate for both the materials and your learners. It is important that you remember that on-line learning has its own unique characteristics that should significantly influence your design.

It is stressed throughout this book and others in the series that the design and development of learning materials should fall into four distinct phases as follows:

1. The initial requirements phase that should include both your materials review and the development of the course information document (CID)

2. Materials design
3. Production
4. Evaluation

On-line learning requirements

During phase 1 you will need to review your current learning materials to identify the new materials that will need to be developed. This review should also clarify the knowledge and skills required by your learners and provide the baseline for the course information document.

As you develop your basic specifications you will also need to identify the required learning objectives along with the standards of performance. This information should also be documented in your course information document.

On-line materials design

The materials design phase should then build on the information you gather in phase 1, along with any external constraints. During this phase you will need to develop a number of appropriate templates for use in the on-line environment. These might include structural, presentation, adaptive and 'how to' tutorials.

A structured learning template simply presents the materials as a hierarchy of topics, one following the other, like a textbook. Here the learner works through the materials in a manner dictated by the designer. It has a standard start page that includes a navigation bar that learners can use to move from one topic page to another, backward and forward.

A presentation learning template is designed to present information in a linear fashion. Presentations can include a slide show or a guided tour. The template should have a standard start page with navigation bar that enables learners to return to the start of the materials at any time.

An adaptive learning template is one that picks the material to be displayed based on information about the learner. This template should be designed so that the learner has no idea that there are other explanations available. The template should also include a standard start page and navigation bar that enables learners to return to the start of the materials at any time.

A how-to learning template helps guide learners though the process of performing a specific task. The structure is usually linear, but some diversions to other templates such as a troubleshooting one can be built in along the way. This type of template can be combined with a reference structure to help learners look up unfamiliar terms.

At the same time as you are developing the templates you should also develop the required tutorial elements such as standard start up pages, structure of elements pages, a consistent set of links and any recap and notes pages.

As you write these design specifications you should assign the required strategies and treatments to the materials along with your assessment methodology. You can also specify various learner utilities at this point.

Finally in this phase of the work you will need to consider a consistent testing and debugging procedure as well as a procedure to help you review the functionality and ease of operation of your 'products'.

The overall design and development of materials for use in an on-line environment is, for the most part, no different from the design and development methodology you have previously employed when developing face-to-face or distance learning materials. The major differences in the design of on-line materials lies in your understanding that your design needs to address four basic issues.

Remember that the 'computer people' should be actively engaged with you in the design of the materials to ensure that they work the way you need them to work.

- **Materials design** – users of on-line learning materials should not just look at the information you present to them, they need to interact with it in novel ways that have no precedents in paper document design. Your materials design must include interaction metaphors, images and concepts to convey function and meaning on the computer screen. In this way your design becomes an integral part of the learner's experience with the learning materials.
- **Organizational design** – there are fundamental organizational reasons for subdividing any large body of information into its component parts. Any body of knowledge to be used in an on-line environment must be designed so that the number of variables is kept to a minimum. This is done using a combination of graphic design and layout conventions along with the division of the information into its discrete units.
- **Page design** – the spatial organization of graphics and text in an on-line environment must help engage your learners in their learning, it must also direct your learner's attention, help them prioritize information and make their interactions more enjoyable and efficient. The on-line learning page shares many similarities to the pages in printed publications but because on-line pages may be accessed directly with little or no preamble, it should be designed

to be more independent than the printed page and not an isolated fragment of information, divorced from the larger context of the parent through the lack of an essential link.

- **Graphic design** – optimizing the look and feel of an on-line learning experience for your learners is important to the overall efficiency of your on-line learning system. The use of a full screen graphic menu and background graphics for example, could leave your learners sitting around waiting for graphics to load. To avoid this you will have to consider a design strategy that draws your learners into the materials with reasonable download times.

Materials production

Materials production should involve two stages. The first is pre-production, where you will have to plan the production itself and carry out, or have others carry out, the actual production of the on-line materials. Production should involve the development of all required graphics along with the development of all of your other required resources.

You will also need to consider some form of formative validation of your materials. This evaluation should be carried out on site by the development team to ensure that the work meets your specifications and is of an acceptable standard.

Once your on-line materials are completed they should be piloted with a small representative sample of your target audience. This evaluation process will help cross-check the performance of your materials against the performance of the objectives and enable any problems to be corrected prior to a full pilot being carried out.

Finally your materials should be taken through an implementation and evaluation phase. You will need to make survey forms, both electronic and paper, available to obtain feedback from your learners and others who use the system. This will help ensure that your materials successfully deliver the right information. Once complete your materials can then go through the cycle again for upgrading purposes and/or to extend their functionality.

The evaluation phase assesses the effectiveness of your learning materials in terms of meeting your stated objectives. The outcome of the evaluation should then feed back into your materials development cycle.

CONCLUSION

This chapter has outlined some of the many issues you will have to consider in the design and development of an on-line learning system. For your system to be a success as both a learning environment and a learning tool you are going to have to take into consideration the various hardware and software needed and available to you. You are also going to have to take into account your own ability to produce the materials and any help you may need with authoring the materials.

Hardware and software links also have to be considered along with the type of environment you want to create. Finally, in the materials development, design and production a number of considerations have to be made to ensure the on-line environment is viable for you both and possibly others as developers and as your learners.

Chapter 9
Issues of Access, Equity and Participation

SUMMARY

The issues of access, equity and participation are not an after-thought. They come from knowing who your audience is likely to be and what their circumstances are. Some of these issues are related to access to resources. Others are related to issues such as discrimination, gender and socio-political or cultural factors. At the very least these factors must be considered so that they are not perpetuated or made worse. More importantly creative solutions need to be developed for those people affected by them.

INTRODUCTION

Much of the information in other parts of this book has to do with access to content and the use of viable learning material. However, there are some other considerations that need to be taken into account when preparing learning materials. In this process, some content experts are able to see the constructs of the subject matter and the relationship within the material very clearly. Often they have ideas how these should be presented. However, these ideas may lead to problems of access, equity and participation in the course. While this could be seen as a planning problem, any possibility of access and equity problems should be eliminated at this course and materials preparation stage.

The main causes of these problems could be eliminated if the content experts considered the varied circumstances of the learners. With some generalization, problems of access, equity and participation can be discussed as follows.

ACCESS

A major consideration is the ability of learners to access any form of education, given the social and political circumstances in which they find themselves.

Increasingly there are considerations of access related to the growth in the use of technology.

- There are problems caused by the need for all participants in a course to have access to sophisticated equipment when the socio-economic situation of some of the participants means this is not feasible.
- There are problems of access to equipment because of gender and/or cultural issues.
- There are problems of access when sophisticated course design and materials require the use of equipment that cannot be easily replicated or supplied elsewhere.
- Access issues arise when some learners are unable to get the same level of information as others of a similar age and ability.

All too frequently materials include references that indicate to some of the learners that they have not been considered. For example, stereotypical gender roles in printed and video materials only serve to reinforce those roles.

Then there are learners with specific needs. Access to the most sophisticated learning is available to people with specific needs, but planning and resource allocation are needed.

What can you do? If nothing else, you can make sure that your programme materials do not make access issues worse.

EQUITY

The issue of equity arises when some seemingly arbitrary (and we emphasize 'seemingly arbitrary') decision denies access to education or aspects of education to one group in the community on grounds other than their ability. Examples still exist but an illustration from the recent past is interesting.

It was not too long ago that some jobs were seen as a male preserve. At the turn of the twentieth century, secretaries were male. However, as the mechanization of the office saw the introduction of the type-writer, dictaphones and, later, word processors, an interesting change occurred. Secretaries became female. Perhaps the men couldn't cope with change. Male secretaries are now sometimes called 'personal assistants' – but can they type? Many are able to use computers... but men are allowed to use computers.

There are also equity issues that can be resolved by recognizing the specific needs of learners.

When you are preparing the materials for your course you will need to consider these equity issues.

PARTICIPATION

Participation issues arise when, for some reason, equally skilled groups are not equally represented in a particular educational activity.

An example from the West has been the differing participation rates of males and females in science. A more significant poor participation rate in mainstream education is found among people with good mental capabilities but physical limitations.

SOME INITIAL OR OBVIOUS PROBLEMS

Language

In the beginning, people used words, grunts and gestures and even a bit of artwork on the sides of caves to communicate with one another. Then people found other people who used different sounds to commu-nicate. This led to the Tower of Babel. (Isn't history simple?) So there are speech problems. These can arise from dialects of the 'same' language or from different languages. Then there are problems of the meaning of words, which are compounded by the ability to read and write the language, which in turn leads to problems of meaning.

Visuals

Visuals have their own problems. We know that photographs can be misleading. We know that editing a set of moving visuals in a particular order can give an entirely different impression, or story, than the same set of visuals presented in another sequence. We also know that computers are capable of altering images. The long and the short of it is that putting together and presenting materials for a course are fraught with problems of access.

PROBLEMS IN REALITY

The language used

Historically there might be a very slim justification for using 'he' when referring to an operator. However, gender-specific references should be avoided whenever possible.

Other examples exist of language that excludes groups. For instance, a section in learning materials labelled 'for managers' could indicate to subordinates (and 'subordinates' is a term that excludes groups) that the information in this section is not for them. However, this is not necessarily so. The section could give them information on why their superior requires information, or the information could be of use in preparing a subordinate for promotion and the tasks and the expectations of the next level of management.

The solution is to examine the material for appropriate language.

The level of language

The book that you are reading is a case in point. We have tried to keep the level of language appropriate.

The solution in preparing the course and the material is to make sure that the complexity of language is appropriate to the subject, the material used in the subject and the expected language ability of the learners.

The complexity of argument

It is easy for a subject expert to write, talk and deliver manuscripts about the content of his or her subject. The problem is that all too often they deal with the material at their own level of expertise.

The solution is to make sure that course development and the materials prepared focus on turning the learner into a knowledgeable person (although perhaps not an expert on the contents of the course).

In face-to-face teaching and traditional correspondence courses, these problems can be illustrated with three examples that can be summed up as a failure to support the learner. These are as follows.

- **Cause and effect** – it seems simple to say that if you put one chemical in a test tube and then put another chemical into the same tube, a reaction occurs and there is a result, for example:

$HCl + H_2O = ?$

The big question is, what happens? However, an equally important question is what happens if you have no understanding of the safety issues in using these chemicals. If you don't know that HCl is hydrogen chloride or hydrochloric acid, and that H_2O represents water, then a simple safety rule about mixing acids and water may be missed.
- **Failing to define terms** – one issue we are aware of in writing these books is that we need to be very clear about the terms we use. For instance, we know that people use terms such as 'objectives' and 'goals' as if they were synonymous. Often people charge into the use of terms and abbreviations without adequate explanation.
- **The use of examples** – examples help unlock the information so long as the example is relevant to the learner. An example outside the learner's experience could lead to confusion. Just consider what you are doing when you ask learners to work through these examples.

ACCESS, EQUITY AND PARTICIPATION: CULTURAL ISSUES

The use of materials in many settings is not without problems related to culture. We as educators must recognize the cultural limitations and work with them. What must be remembered is that change is possible; we should be developing materials that are better, not worse.

The prime concern of anyone developing material is that the issues raised by cultural differences are addressed. At the very least, the following considerations should be taken into account.

- Take care with the use of language so that where men and women are capable and allowed to do the same job, the terms applied do not indicate a gender (usually male) bias.

- Make sure that the role models used in the materials, particularly photos and video material, adequately represent the opportunities for all in society to contribute.
- Consider the options of delivery of courses. Courses offered in the middle of the day may be open to those without other commitments, but may prevent certain groups attending. The same course offered at a different time may see the target audience for the course expand.
- In some maths and science courses it has been found that the participation rate of females increases in the absence of males. This was found to be related to the way in which males dominated any discussion at the expense of females. (What it does for their social life is another matter.)
- If any level of technology is involved, do some study to determine if the basic technology is available. (Many companies are now using interactive communication technology, which is more expensive than an airmail postage stamp, but cheaper and faster than an international jet, and costs little more than an IDD call. The equipment required is available but at a cost that only corporations can support; what about the humble learners?)
- Some subjects demand that computers are available. This is fine if they are also needed for the job, and/or for long-term participation in the course. If a computer is only needed for a relatively short time, it will be an added cost burden that may deter people from enrolling. The tool is effectively denying access.

There is a further consideration to do with assessment, which needs to be addressed at the preparation stage.

Briefly, assessment tasks need to be appropriate to the course, reflect the material presented in the course and relate to the expected outcomes. In most schools the timing of assessment is not an issue, but in post-compulsory courses assessment tasks under controlled conditions may cause problems.

Assessment tasks should be timed to occur at the same or similar time as classes or courses. Do not expect night- or evening-class students to attend an assessment during the day. They may have to take leave, which can add stress and is something day students do not have to do. In practice this could mean that a learner completes the course but, without access to equipment or an assessment centre, they are unable to undertake – or pass – the assessment. By default, you are placing these night/evening students under different conditions; this is not equitable.

ACCESS, EQUITY AND PARTICIPATION: TECHNOLOGY

The move towards more open learning structures using technology as a delivery tool also raises concerns for those involved in the preparation of materials for delivery.

The idea of developing a course that requires technological support sounds fine in theory, particularly if it allows the learner some control over the information flow and their learning. The problem arises when there is no access to technology. This does not first apply to economically-disadvantaged areas or groups. In many countries, educational institutions' budgets cannot support sophisticated delivery mechanisms. Even if technology is available, access may be restricted for other reasons, such as limited availability of machines, causing rationing of access, or an adequate number of machines, but without the appropriate peripheral devices.

At the time of writing, the best example is from computing, where the move to multimedia means that even comparatively new machines appear obsolete because they do not have CD ROM players or there are RAM or hard disk limitations. (Without becoming too involved... typically, 10 MBytes of RAM isn't enough to run most applications, while hard disks of 80 MBytes are now barely adequate.)

The use of technology is becoming more available to learners, when they can afford it or when teachers feel it is not a threat to their role.

You will need to consider that if the technology is so fragile, perhaps it has not been designed for an educational and training setting. One example in the training setting is the need to show a video to help explain a process, yet many of the video recorders are not equipped to work in a factory or workshop environment. The same is true of computers. Computers and video equipment are designed to work in relatively clean surroundings. They have vents to assist in cooling; in a workshop these same vents allow dust to enter. One solution is to have a clean room nearby, but this adds to the cost.

Technophobia

There are still people who hope that if they ignore technology it will go away. There is another group of people who understand the need for technology and would like it to have a place in their lives, but have a fear of using it.

If you are involved in preparing new courses and course materials you must consider what effect the use of technology may have on the learner and prepare the materials to take this into account.

WHERE DO I START?

If you have an interest in the Internet you may have visited a number of educational sites to check out the available information. Examples of the kind of information you find are course outlines. To be really meaningful this information needs to be interpreted. The first question is what information your Internet site provides. Let me provide an example from the learner's point of view.

As a learner I am looking for a course in a particular topic area. Through the Internet I do a search. The results of the search show that there are four courses in this topic in the world. I then want to refine my search to determine which of these courses is geographically close, the least expensive and the most prestigious. The results of this search are that three out of the four institutions have simply put their handbook/course calendar on the Internet with little or no further information. As a potential learner I find this frustrating. The consequence of this is that I make no further enquiry.

The fourth institution has developed their course and used the latest Internet browser with full digital sound and video that is incompatible with all of the applications on my computer. The result there is that I can't access the learning so I sign up for a class in welding. This class requires that I attend at nominated times over a period of time and I am issued with a set of class notes. I complete the course and receive a certificate.

The course provider has different needs

What is my need or 'Why do I want to put a course on the Internet?' To properly answer this question you will need to do an analysis of what it is you want to put on the Internet.

At the very least you may decide to put up the course brochure, the calendar of courses offered or information about your institution. Even this will require a rethink of how the material is designed so that the features of the course(s) are promoted.

On an Internet site the best way of doing this is to take into account the nature of the delivery tool and HTML and scan in a brochure or information.

At the other end of the continuum is the need to place course materials on an Internet site for learners to access. In this situation you have extended the learners' access to your site from mere information to enabling the learner to 'chat' with course advisors and the enrolling centre. You may develop a registration site with the capability to accept the electronic transfer of funds to cover course cost. Associated with this will be a site where the enrolled learner now has access to the course information and the related support services. These support services should include at the very least, a 'tutorial' and 'feedback'. This is only an indication of the need for sophisticated thinking about information supply and learner support.

There are other factors that come into play when considering the Internet as a means of delivery. One of the main considerations is the issue of access and equity. Again it is a position on a continuum. At one end is a huge multinational company with a need and the communication infrastructure to support education and training in remote locations. At the other end are people without access.

The expenditure of effort to provide course materials at any point on the continuum has to be based on a realistic appraisal of the likely outcomes. It could be that providing access has a greater impact in an under-serviced setting than servicing the needs of the multinational. The outcomes in terms of developing the learners could be the same, however, it happens in a different environment.

Underlying this is the assumption that the Internet is a delivery mechanism that has built-in applications to transform existing information into learning materials.

Redesign of existing materials

As stated previously, it is believed by some that existing course material is easily translated onto an Internet site.

The reality is quite different, and the expectations of people accessing sites are evolving. The current use of Internet course material indicates that there are at least three sets of users. The first set are the those who sign on and are at the front of the class seeking exposure. The second set are those that surf the options. Then there is the third set, who sample the course information or even the course itself but are essentially sitting at the back of the class.

The question then arises about redesigning the course as it is clear that with the three different audiences it is not simply a matter of dumping face-to-face class material into an Internet acceptable application. Real work is required to make sure that:

- learners' needs are meet
- the security of the course material is maintained

● those enrolled are the students submitting the assessment material.

In redesigning course material for Internet delivery there are real questions about preparing the material, the form that this delivery will take and the evaluation process.

Over a period of time the cycle of course information seems to be getting shorter, with course information and course content changing to cope with the influence of technology. As an educator or trainer within an institution (public or private) the accountability, appropriateness and relationship to client/learner need is becoming more critical in terms of the rapid response needed. Along with this rapid response is the increasing need to customize material at an enterprise level rather than at an industry wide level. This is based on the speculation that small to medium sized companies and the start-up and spin-off companies from research organizations may not have the ability to generate their own training.

Large or mature companies with their own internal computer based or Intranet capabilities will use these means in the belief that it maintains their competitive edge.

In many parts of the computer based education world it would seem that the need to deliver courses via the Internet is a requirement for both academic and/or technological credibility. Having visited sites offering courses, even at the lower level of course information, there are two conclusions.

The first is that the site developers do not have any idea about computer screen design and the second is that there is a real question on most sites about the input from anyone with educational experience.

The result is that all or any effort by the people who developed the sites has been a waste of time. They may have recorded a hit, in that my visit to the site is recorded, but the big miss is that I will not return to that site again, unless my short-term memory fails.

DELIVERY OPTIONS

The part of my life dealing with educational technology has for many years been governed by the need for appropriate use of technology in education and training.

My work experience in the use of technology to support education and training began with programmed learning, moved through the evolution of film to video and the development of video cassettes through to computer based learning, satellite and interactive on-line learning to the current fashion of the Internet and Intranet as a tool for delivery. During these years I have developed the following operational question: what does the technology have to offer?

In cases such as distance education if the technology enhancing interaction and support for learning is available, I am a willing supporter. However, I am seeing in the late 1990s that developers of technology are still using the education and training sector as the first port of call for marketing the new technology product.

The reality is that the developers of technology and educational technologists end up in an alliance attempting to prove the educational or training edge. In many cases the options of using existing technologies or minimal technology are overlooked. In preparing the course materials the delivery options are overlooked.

PREPARING LEARNING MATERIALS

If you are still intent on preparing course material for Internet delivery then there are several important questions you must ask.

- What Internet site development resources do I have?
- How will be this be supported?
- What content expertise is needed to develop the learning materials?
- What is the content expertise to support the teaching and learning?
- What is the availability of this expertise?

Selecting prepared learning materials

It is assumed that there are tools available to translate word processing files into web pages readily. The reality is that most of these translation packages only result in scrollable Internet pages with few if any interaction points. For the user this means hit the scroll bar, not beam me up into higher levels of information.

A consequence of this is that the use of existing materials needs to go through a process of analysis. The purpose of the analysis should be to determine what is appropriate for delivery via the Internet and what other support services are needed.

For example, there could be courses in the information technology (IT) and computing area that are suited to total or almost complete delivery via the Internet, because they are part of the skills upgrade required for continued work in the IT industry. Then there are courses in other areas where it might be appropriate to provide course outlines and readings or simulation exercises on the Internet. These, along with others, will require a less or greater degree of face-to-face contact. There may well be some courses that are not suitable for Internet delivery. This should be recognized and any attempt to force fit the course to Internet delivery rigorously opposed.

The criteria for selecting material for Internet delivery includes applicability to Internet delivery, interactivity, stability of information over a period of time to 'recoup investment' in the establishing of the site, page/screen size, platform, committed ongoing site maintenance (particularly in content that is rapidly changing), teaching staff committed to a 24-hour turn around seven days a week during the period of enrolment, flexible enrolment, faculty and institution.

CONCLUSION

Issues of access, prior learning and so on should be addressed at the planning stage to ensure that appropriate courses and materials are developed.

Chapter 10
The Independent Learner

SUMMARY

What is an independent learner? There is an assumption that independent learners need a certain level of maturity, yet people of all ages demonstrate an ability to learn independently of a formal system of learning and independently within education and training systems. This chapter looks at some assumptions about characteristics and learners.

INTRODUCTION

In most teaching, learning and training settings there is either a stated or implied objective that as a result of the course, study, or training, the learner will use the new information or skills in appropriate settings. This is based on an assumption that the learner will be able to work independently after they are introduced to new knowledge or skills and their operating parameters.

In preparing materials for learners and to encourage independence, there are times when you will want to build in activities which promote the learners' confidence in using the new knowledge or skills. In doing so, you are giving the learner a message about their independence. However, all too frequently this message of independence is then quashed if the outcome produced by the learner is not as the teacher intended.

In planning a course and course materials to foster independent learning, what are the criteria that you can use? There are huge arguments over how people learn, or what constitutes learning, as shown

Learning is a human process. It's about making sense of the learning experience. Review your materials to ensure that they make sense.

by the range of terms used: rote learning; experiential learning; teaching from simple facts to complex relationship of content; teaching concrete statements to abstract considerations; the expectation of competence or the construction of meaning.

There is also the view that learning takes place within a construct that represents reality and influences how course content is considered, presented and the learners' reaction treated. This presentation of course information will differ if it is based on a certain religious tradition, within a particular political climate or if it attempts to put across a specific world view to the learners.

GENERAL USES OF THE TERM 'INDEPENDENT LEARNER'

Sometimes the term 'independent learner' is used to refer to people learning through distance education or in 'off-campus' modes. This independence is a reflection of these learners' need for flexibility in study. In reality, many of the courses studied off-campus have a rigid time frame for enrolment and the completion of assignments, with the result that the learner might be physically dependent on or constrained by the 'administrative requirements' of the institution.

Frequently the term 'independent learner' is associated with the maturity of the learner. Often this maturity has little to do with chronological age. Sometimes the term is a misnomer for the educational or training process because the learning is often very dependent on the material they use, or the ability to be certified as a result of their studies, or meeting the standards set for recognition of completion of the course.

An alternative view

Educational psychologists and cognitive scientists consider that independent learning could be seen as starting at birth. Parents and caregivers will recognize that a new-born infant is learning, because he or she seems to know how to gain attention through a cry, and how to operate and trigger learning responses in the parents or carers such as 'feed me' and 'change me'.

In many educational settings learners are set tasks either as projects, homework, or assignments. Some learners set their own learning goals. The issue then arises of how teachers balance the role of giving the learner independence to go about the task, with the need to monitor the task, its progress and what the possible outcomes might be in relation to the teacher's expectations, the objectives of the course and the outcomes for the learners.

Changes in education and training

In presenting a very brief and selected history of education and training in the last 40 years, the following points can be made as generalizations. The first is that there has been a change from education for a job for life to education that might get you a job. The second is that this job may disappear even as you are employed. The third is that you will need to be retrained or have your current skills recognized before you become employed again. The fourth is that learning is now a lifelong activity. The truism that you 'learn a new thing every day' is a reality. This 'new thing' may just give you the edge in gaining a job or promotion.

What then do we mean by the term 'independent learner'?

Simply put, an independent learner is one who is to a greater or lesser extent able to develop and express a learning goal and undertake actions to achieve that goal. This indicates that the learner is operating at a level where they know what they want to know and how to achieve it. This is meta-cognition. The actions may be nothing more than asking another to tell them what they want to know. This could be a teacher, a parent or carer or even a peer. At a more complex level, the learner could use a set of skills to undertake an enquiry using a set of criteria that the learner has determined. This could be called 'meta-learning'.

Help your learners by keeping the learning materials as simple as possible. Help learners apply everyday approaches to the business of learning.

The idea of being an independent learner has a connection with the promotion of personal initiative. More importantly, it is about the development of people who are capable of saying that was yesterday and this is my tomorrow. And there are possibly different tomorrows, as employment opportunities will differ in the future.

PROMOTING INDEPENDENCE

If education and training are about developing in the learner the skills for them to go about the task of satisfying their own needs effectively, in part this is because of the culture of lifelong learning. In part it is to do with learners being the best people to decide what, in the vast spread of knowledge and skills available, they want to learn and what they need to learn. Sometimes these are two different expectations, but they are not mutually exclusive.

Following from this there would seem to be three types of independent learners. These are:

- naive learners
- those being weaned off institutional education
- just-in-time learners.

Naive learners

Learning starts early. In the current literature it is suggested that learning starts even before a baby is born. (No, it is not suggested that a foetus could sit down and work out fractal theorems.) Teachers in education and training tend to forget that learners have a huge experience in reacting to their environment and learning from that environment before they experience formal education and training. At all stages in the education and training process teachers greet their new learners as though this were the first time that the learner has come in contact with formal education or training. The rites of passage from primary education to secondary, or from secondary to tertiary education often ignore much of the prior learning. Perhaps this is too harsh. It may be more correct to say that among the teachers at the various levels of education there is a lack of communication about the tasks that the learners achieved, apart from the results recorded in the official documentation, and perhaps it is the documentation that is at fault.

It could be argued that the young learner often has the enthusiasm or curiosity for learning taken away by the need to conform to a formal education system.

What needs to be promoted is how to prolong the inquisitiveness of the naive learner, because learners are never fully naive.

Those being weaned off institutional education

That many learners become locked into the institutional mode of learning is understandable. In part, alternative models such as distance education try to mirror the requirements of learning in a formal setting.

How then can we go about promoting independence? The first thing that needs to be considered is how locked into a process is the learner.

The independent learner is often independent of time as well – the learner decides when he or she wants to learn. This would not be possible in the formal setting of education and training, with the year broken up into terms or semeseters, as someone expressing an interest in a subject half-way through a semester is not going to fit into the administrative requirements, let alone the teaching pattern already established. The predominance of 'administrative convenience' over-looks the fact that the client is the learner.

There are several strategies that can be used to promote independence and perhaps overcome administrative inflexibility.

The use of contracts

Under a contract, the learner does something within an agreed frame-work. The objectives and outcomes are negotiated, the time frame of the contract is agreed, and the expectation of the parties involved is spelt out.

The use of reports

While the outcome may be the same as a contract, in a report the learner establishes the action to be taken and within his/her restraints provides information on the outcomes of his/her actions.

The use of mentors

Here again the actual outcome may be no different from the contract. However, in the initial stages of mentoring there is often a teacher: learner relationship, often referred to in academic books as a 'cognitive apprenticeship'. Trade training and apprenticeships have been with us for a long while. In the traditional apprenticeship, not only did the skills have to be learned; there was also a time-serving component. With mentoring, the skills need to be learned but the notion of time-serving is replaced with the recognition of skills learned. In other words, the time taken will be the time needed, not some arbitrarily determined length of time. Another feature of mentoring is the need to support the learner during the initial sessions. After this initial period of close supervision, and as the teacher/master sees that the learner/apprentice is becoming familiar with and proficient at the task, the teacher/master begins a process of fading away, but always remaining in the background until such time as the knowledge, skills and attitudes of the learner/apprentice match those of the teacher/master.

Just-in-time learners

Review the needs of your learners and determine the best time for your materials to be delivered to them. It might just boost attendance in your class!

Just-in-time learning refers to education and training taking place when it is needed, and reskilling and skills development that takes place when jobs become obsolete and different jobs emerge. Just-in-time education and training happens when learners are ready to move into a new phase of their education and/or training.

Coping with just-in-time learners

Just-in-time learners can turn up in any educational and training setting. The problem that they create is how to handle their demands for their present needs. The answer is a bit of a 'cop out' but the needs are met by maintaining a good feel for what's happening in education, in training and in industry and employment.

An example: 30 years ago, who would have said stone masonry was needed? In today's world of restoration and appreciation of historical buildings, the stone mason's craft is thriving. Of equal importance is the survival of the trades that support the stone mason, such as foundry crafts like tool-making.

IDENTIFICATION OF NEEDS

There is a need to respond to requests from learners. It may be that what they express as a need is not what they require, but to dismiss these expressions without negotiation could lead to you and the learner being worse off. The identification of need and the satisfaction of that need is a matter of negotiation.

ENROLMENT AND RECOGNITION OF PRIOR LEARNING

You may need to consider recognition of prior learning. The most difficult aspect of this is recognizing life experiences as part of a credit towards completing a course.

An example might serve to make the point. A person enrols in a book-keeping course. How do you recognize the fact that this person has been treasurer for a local sporting team for the last six years?

CERTIFICATION

The course that the independent learner completes may require certification. As always there are two certification processes: the first is to certify that the course and exemptions will be recognized by the certi-fication body; the second is to validate that the learner completed the requirements and is therefore 'certificated'.

SOME WORDS OF WARNING

If you are considering placing a learner on a non-traditional path it is your duty to ensure that the learner can complete the course and be recorded as successful by the 'authorities'.

To make sure this does happen, let's step back from the situation and ask one question: did you have the authority, agreement, sanction, and/or negotiating rights to offer an alternative to the learner in the first place? If the answer is no then possibly you have been negligent.

There may be a requirement for the learner to do extra work. In some educational and training settings, being able to prove you are capable in any way other than using the traditional methods raises the suspicion that the qualification is being gained easily. To overcome this accusation, some organizations grant alternative methods of completing a course or gaining a qualification, but impose such an overload of other conditions that many people give up. People giving up a course is a waste of resource. What do you do when such an over-load is imposed or threatened?

CONCLUSION

When learners take part in a course and participate in developing the course they need, there is a widespread suspicion, some of it on very good grounds, that a learner doing a course by non-standard means is somehow getting an easy option. That this learner has taken the risk of stepping outside the traditional model of education, risking their credibility as a learner, is rarely taken into consideration. The consid-eration is for the credibility of the awarding institution. This under-pins the award granted to the learner. You as teacher in an institution could also feel under threat if accommodating the independent learner does not yield good results.

Chapter 11

Preparing to Deliver an Innovation

SUMMARY

When developing new materials, the processes that you need to go through to prepare the learners and the wider community for their delivery are often overlooked. What are some of the pitfalls of introducing new courses or materials and how can they be avoided?

(The information in this chapter is supported by further information in the third book in this series, dealing with 'Delivery'.)

INTRODUCTION

You have done all this planning and preparation; what else can you do to optimize success? In other chapters we have mentioned the need to include the education and training community in making decisions about changes in the education and training process. However, does this mean they are ready to accept change? You must remember that people are used to hearing about change, and you've probably heard the term, 'Not in my lifetime'. But what are these people going to do when it does happen in their lifetime?

This chapter discusses aspects of preparing to deliver in relation to the learners and the community supporting the learners and their understanding of:

- the innovation or change
- the need to develop time frames
- developing and maintaining support
- some of the blocks
- induction.

CHANGE

The issue you must keep before the education and training community you work within is not just one of the change; this will at best see limited support. You have to assure the community that the change *will* take place. At the same time as you discuss that the change will happen, the community must be convincing in their support for the change when it happens. To make the community consider change seriously, you should start to talk in time frames.

To make change happen you will have to get the right people involved.

TIME FRAMES

Time frames are interesting: there will be your time frame, probably getting the change underway as soon as possible; then there will be the time frame of the community; in fact there may be many time frames. Some of these could belong to traditionalists who, for different reasons, may say, 'not in my time'; or to the timid who will say 'soon'; and then you could have those enthusiasts who cannot understand why everyone wasn't doing this course or using these materials yesterday.

It is important for the time frame to be understood. If it isn't, then timid supporters may become vocal detractors if they see the changes offered by the new course or materials as being introduced too fast. The optimists may see these same changes as taking place too slowly and this will cause them to become critical. The end result is conflict over implementation or delivery, which detracts attention from the delivery itself.

In the preparation stage for the course and/or materials you must be aware that an inflexible time frame can lead to difficulties if unforeseen circumstances arise. For example, the inability of a time frame to cope with your illness or an illness among team members could cause problems. However, flexible time frames can cause problems of their own. For example, an attempt to allow for illness or other absence could place pressure on other members of the team. You must remember that while one exception breaks the rule it also makes a rule: the exception breaks the rule that time frames are to be followed; it makes the rule that time frames can be treated as waste paper basket lining.

DEVELOPING AND MAINTAINING SUPPORT

Developing and maintaining support for the introduction of a new course or development of course material can be achieved if all those in the team or all those directly affected by any necessary time frame change are informed. The effect on the old time frame must then be documented and the resulting modification accepted.

One could hope that these changes are minimal; after all, the planning and preparation activities are meant to uncover the unforeseen and to predict the unexpected. However, an educational organization is a people organization. This means that adjustments or fine tuning are acceptable so long as all who need to know are informed.

THE BLOCKS

The question that must asked again is: do you consider that you have done all the work? The process you have gone through may well have included very heavy issues such as task analysis. It will probably have included a study to determine the best means of addressing the problem and providing a solution. It should include information on the learners, or the community that the learners will possibly come from, as this will provide you with further information on potential sources of blocks to the change process. This is the material you collected on the Course Information Document (CID) and associated documents.

Change is difficult so it makes sense for you to assess just how difficult it will be for you to push it through.

... to new education and training

Teachers are constantly fine-tuning the teaching and training practices they use. In part this is to account for variations the teachers recognize among the learners; in part it is caused by new information or techniques arising that must be incorporated if the teaching and learning process is to remain relevant to the needs of the learners. We would expect that this would happen without becoming a block. However, when new courses and materials are introduced, there are issues or blocks that can emerge.

... to a new course or course materials

What follows are several real-life examples of new initiative which ran into problems.

Example 1: full-ahead on change without a pilot or consultation
Real blocks emerge when major changes are attempted without piloting or consultation.

Consider the concern and anger raised among learners, parents and carers if, in the middle of preparation for final exams, a minister of education announced that the system of marking and moderating exams for entrance into university would be changed.

Whether the changes the minister sought to make were applicable, valid or warranted would be forgotten. Here were students in the middle of preparing for exams being told that the rules of marking and reporting were to be changed.

In one such case, thousands of upset students, supported by equally confused and angry parents, marched on parliament.

The innovation foundered because there was a lack of communication with the educational community.

Example 2: raised or misplaced expectations within the team
As a teacher you see an opportunity to include a new material or organize a course a bit differently. If you are the only teacher and the changes do not violate the curriculum then there is little problem. But what happens if other teachers are involved either within the institution or across the nation?

There is a difficult block that emerges very late in the process. The very action of exploring an area for improvement can spark off support and ideas, but opening up options leads to people extending their expectations. By making some things possible, further options are also seen as being possible, so at the last moment someone will ask what about doing this or adding that to the course or course materials. The team has moved away from satisfying the needs of the user.

To deal with this you may have to rely on course documentation to rationally excluded these 'new' suggestions. However, the suggestions should be noted for possible inclusion in subsequent course or materials reviews.

Example 3: raised or misplaced expectations in the clients' community
Parents have been to school. Some remember this as a good experience, others remember school with less positive thoughts. Most

parents not involved in education and training have not seen the change in the educational paradigm from the industrial model of education and training for a job to the new paradigm of life-long education and training.

Given that changes in the world at large are rapid and frequent, it is sometimes surprising that when it comes to education and training there is an expectation that nothing has changed, or that change is very slow. The saying, 'That was the way that we did it when I went to school', is based on a feeling that if learning and training is easier these days, it cannot be as comprehensive or rigorous as it was in previous times. The derivative assumption is that today's learning and training must be inferior. This is perhaps understandable, but the arrival of computing provides an exception.

Computers are not a panacea, but they can help people complete calculations and many other tasks that were once very time-consuming. Even amongst the very young, the use of computers is encouraged in class and to prepare assignments. However, what does the wider community expect?

For instance, electronic calculators and abacuses are examples of calculators. So too are fingers, thumbs and toes. That some of these tools could be excluded from an exam setting seems a nonsense. If you take any or all of these tools into an exam then you will need to know how to use them in order to arrive at the 'correct' result. However, if not all students have access to the same set of equipment during the same exam then access and equity issues arise. The wider expectation of the community is that all learners will experience similar learning experiences in the same course, however seldom we know this occurs in practice.

Example 4: ongoing support
This can be a real block. In one sense the problem is not getting the support but how to lock-in that support. Five sets of actions can assist. Many of these will have been considered during planning, but there is a need to make sure they happen during preparation.

1. As far as your expectations and the expectations of the community are concerned, the advice here is to keep everyone informed.
2. Reporting. Plan your reporting process and make sure that the people involved and the community know that you will be reporting to them.
3. The launch. The real question here is, do you have one or do you just let things happen? The need for a launch will be dictated by the

size of the project or the cost of developing the materials. A change in classroom activity probably happens with little fanfare and is 'announced' in discussion with colleagues over a cup of tea or coffee.

A formal launch for new materials often takes place when real money is involved, or there are sponsors who are seeking publicity for themselves as much as for the materials, or when the materials have some wider significance, such as regional or national application. In the latter case, the launch will need to be attended not only by the key players involved in the development but community leaders and politicians with responsibility for education and training.

It is difficult to determine an exact list given the different situations, but if the materials you have developed are significant, the department, college, education or training authority will be aware of your work and you may well be approached about a launch, well before you are ready.

4. Monitoring. If the materials are within your area of supervision then monitoring will be a natural happening. You will want to find out how your materials are going.
5. Data collection. It was noted above that you might need to collect information on the implementation and the effect of the materials. You need to consider how to do this without it causing you too many headaches and becoming too daunting a task.

A problem arises with material for wider distribution. How have you planned or prepared for ensuring that the materials are used as intended and how are you going to find out if others are having 'problems' with the materials? You will have to prepare some feedback mechanisms. At a sophisticated level this could be a 'hot line' or, at a less sophisticated level, you might consider incorporating a feedback form in the materials and invite users to fill it in and return it to you.

Sometimes others have problems using materials that they have not devised themselves; this may be caused by a lack of confidence. In such a situation your materials may not be fully utilized. You will have to decide if this matters and what you will do about it.

INDUCTION

As a final preparation task, consider if you will need to induct, train, or provide support for the users. If you do, it would be better before rather than after the introduction of the new materials. A short induction programme may be out of the question because of budget constraints, but a simple kit to guide users on the use of the new materials may be feasible.

What you are trying to avoid is people using the materials and not liking them. This should not happen if the initial information collected on the course specification form has been followed. However, there will always be some who will consider that they could do better, or even that what they have now is better. This may be a consultation problem, or petty jealousy. You will need to take care that any friction caused does not develop into opposition and denigration of the materials.

CONCLUSION

In preparing to deliver a new course or new course materials, the planning process needs to be checked to make sure that delivery will be as smooth as possible. This involves:

- recognizing and preparing for any threat caused by the change
- developing time frames that are understood by the key players and stakeholders
- developing strategies to make sure that support is sustained
- considering some of the blocks to the next stage of delivery
- conducting an induction programme that recognizes the concerns of the key players and stakeholders.

Further Reading

Briggs, L J, Gustafson, K L, Tillman, M H (eds) (1991) *Instructional Design. Principles and Applications*, 2nd edn, Englewood Cliffs, NJ: Educational Technology Publications.

Clennell, S, Peters, J and Sewart, D (1988) 'Teaching for the open university', in *Distance Education: International Perspectives*, Sewart, D, Keegan, D and Holmberg, B, eds, London: Routledge, pp 327–38.

Dick, W and Reiser, R A (1989) *Planning Effective Instruction*, London: Allyn and Bacon.

Dorrell, J (1993) *Resource-based Learning, Using Open and Flexible Learning Resource for Continuous Development*, Maidenhead: McGraw-Hill.

Ellington, H (1985) *Producing Teaching Materials*, London: Kogan Page.

Ellington, H and Race, P (1992) *Producing Teaching Materials*, 2nd edn, London: Kogan Page.

Evans, T (ed.) (1990) *Research in Distance Education 1*, Institute of Distance Education, Deakin University, Deakin University Press.

Gagné, R M (1977) *Conditions of Learning*, 3rd edn, New York: Holt, Rinehart & Winston.

Gagné, R M, Briggs, L J and Wager, W W (1992) *Principles of Instructional Design*, 4th edn, London: Harcourt Brace Jovanovich.

Gentry, C G (1994) Introduction to Instructional Development. *Process and Technique*, Belmont, Ca: Wadsworth Publishing.

Gibbs, G, Habeshaw, S and Habeshaw, T (1988) *53 Interesting Things to Do in Your Lectures*, Bristol: Technical and Educational Services.

Gibbs, G, Habeshaw, S and Habeshaw, T (1988) *53 Interesting Things to Do in Your Seminars and Tutorials*, Bristol: Technical and Educational Services.

Holmberg, B (1980) *Essentials of distance education.* (A course on distance education) Fernuniversitat, Hagen: ZIFF.

Holmberg, B (1989) *Theory and practice of distance education*, London: Routledge.

Keegan, D (1990) *Foundations of distance education*, 2nd edn, London: Routledge.

Kemp, E (1980) *Planning and Producing Audio Visual Material*, New York: Harper and Row.

Lewis, R (1985) *How to Develop and Manage an Open-learning Scheme*, Open Learning Guide 5, Council for Educational Technology, London: Charlesworth.

Lewis, R and Spencer, D (1986) *What is Open Learning?*, Open Learning Guide 4, Council for Educational Technology, London: Charlesworth.

Majorbanks, K (ed.) (1991) *The Foundations of Students' Learning*, New York: Pergamon Press.

Marland, P, Patching, W, Putt, I and Putt, R (1990) 'Distance learners' interaction with text while studying', *Distance Education*, volume 11, number 1, pp 71–91.

Race, P (1989) *The Open Learning Handbook – Selecting, Designing and Supporting Open Learning Materials*, London: Kogan Page/Nichols.

Rowntree, D (1990) *Teaching through Self-instruction*, revised edn, London: Kogan Page.

Rowntree, D (1982) *Exploring Open and Distance Learning, Open and Distance Learning Series*, Milton Keynes: The Open University.

Staff Development and Educational Methods Unit, Manchester Polytechnic (1979) *Designs for Teaching, Small Group Teaching*, Council for Educational Technology.

Wilson, B (1987) *Methods of Training and Individualised Instruction*, Volume 3, Training technology programme, Carnforth: Parthenon Publishing.

Wilson, B (1987) *Methods of Training: Groupwork*, Volume 2, Training technology programme, Carnforth: Parthenon Publishing.

Index

assessment   55, 110
assignments   31–32
audio tapes   37

blueprints see teacher-
    independent
teaching materials
brainstorming   12
buzz groups   12

case study   49
CD Rom   24, 75, 98, 111
certification   122–23
classroom discussions   10
cognitive apprenticeship   121
computer-based materials
    41–44
computer-based training   (CBT)
    16, 75
computer-managed learning
    (CML)   16, 75, 91, 96
computer simulation   39
computers see Internet, on-line
    learning, technology
correspondence education   16
course documentation   48
course information document
    (CID)   21, 35, 60, 61, 72, 74,
    79, 100, 101, 126

course notes   48
course support document   57–58
course units   24–33
    assignments   31–32
    design   24–25
    field trial   33
    page layout   27–29
    planning   25–27
    self-help questions   29–31
cultural change   83–84
    see also innovation
curriculum document   20

directed private study   16
distance education   19–33, 75,
    115, 120
    course design   20–25
    course units   24–31
    development model   22
    development team   20
    definition   19
    field trial of materials   33
    modular   23
distance learning   4, 14

education
    access to 106
    equity 106–07
    participation of learners   107

Educational Research
    Association   38
English Teachers Association
    38
evaluation
    teaching materials/resources
        59–69

field trips   12
flexible learning   4, 16

games   12
graphic user interface (GUI)
    100
group instruction   8–12, 81
    large group work   10
    objectives   9–10
    role of teacher   17–18
    small group work   11–12
    tutorials   10–11

home study   16, 98

illustrations   26–27
independent learning   117–23
    preparing course materials
        117–18
    types of learner   120–22
individualized instruction
    13–16, 81
    role of teacher   17
innovation
    attitudes   85–87
    blocks to   126–29
    cultural change   83–84, 124
    implementation strategies
        84–85, 88–90, 94
    induction of users   129–30
    involving learners   93
    participation   87–88
    preparing to deliver   124–30
    staff development   86–87

teacher support   88–89, 126
time frames   125–26
instruction
    events of   54–55
    group   8–12
    individualized   13–16
    learning process   118
    mass   5–8
instructional designer   20–21
    see also distance education
instructional materials
    see teaching materials
interactive lecture notes   7–8
interactive video   4, 16
Internet   24, 42, 112, 113–16
    see also on-line learning,
        technology

KIS ('keep it simple')   34, 38–39,
    44, 98

language   107, 108–09
learner contracts   121
learner profile   21, 23
learner reports   121
learners
    assessment   110
    barriers to education
        105–16
    identification of needs   12
    independent   117–23
learning event sheets   48, 49,
    50
    checking   56
    sequencing   52–54
learning process *see* instruction,
    lifelong learning
lectures *see* mass instruction
lesson plans   48, 49, 51
lifelong learning   119
local area network (LAN)   95,
    98

mass instruction   5–8, 37, 81
 lectures   5–6
 role of teacher   17
mastery learning   4, 16
materials *see* teaching materials
mentors   121
meta-cognition   119
meta-learning   119
multi-media programs   99

on-line classroom   96–97, 99
on-line learning   95–104
 design and development
  100–03
 production   103
 programs   99
 software categories   97–98
 tutorials   101–02
open learning   13, 82, 89–93
 application   14–15
 information   90–91
 packages   15–16
 role of teacher   89
organizational culture   82–83
 see also cultural change
overheads   39, 40

performance objectives   23, 24
photographs   24, 27, 107
prior learning   122
production
 companies   73
 in-house   73
 on-line learning materials   103
 plan 76–78
 teaching materials   70–80
programme learning   16
pupils *see* learners

resource-appraisal techniques
  66–67
resource-based learning   4, 16

resources *see* teaching materials
research exercise   37
role plays   12, 37, 49
ROPES   56

self-help questions   29–31
self-test questions   33
seminars   11
simulations   12, 37
small group discussion   12, 37,
  49
software
 client   97–98
 server   97–98
 support   97–98
students *see* learners
suggested readings   48
supported study   16

teacher
 roles of   16–18
teacher-independent learning
  materials   45–58
 approaches   47–48
teaching materials
 development   45–58
 innovation   81–94
 on-line learning   95–104
 page layout   27–30
 preparation   34–44
 production   70–80, 103
 selection criteria   59–69
 specification   74–76
 see also on-line learning,
  teacher-independent
  learning materials,
  technology
teaching notes   39, 41
technology
 access to 106, 110, 111
 teaching aids   36–38, 41–44,
  53, 114–15, 128

see also computers, Internet,
 on-line learning
technophobia   111
terminology   109
text formatting   27–28
time lines   76, 92
tutorials   10–11, 37

video   24, 37, 39, 40, 75, 111

video disks   24
virtual classroom   95
visual presentation   37, 107–08

wide area network (WAN)   97
workbooks   37, 39, 75
worked examples   37
workshop   37
World Wide Web   13, 95